"Todd Nesloney and Adam Welcome are extraordinary educators who go above and beyond to uplift, motivate, support, and educate every student. Just imagine how all children would thrive if we all would remember to do the same. With Todd and Adam, kids always come first! *Kids Deserve It!* is a must read."

Kim Bearden, @KimBearden, educator, speaker, co-founder of The Ron Clark Academy and author of Crash Course: The Life Lessons My Students Taught Me

"In *Kids Deserve It!*, Todd Nesloney and Adam Welcome challenge educators to remember why they got into this business in the first place, and to harness the passion that first drove them to want to make a difference in the lives of young people. He further challenges us and to be brave in the face of people and policies that sometimes make it difficult to put kids first. Through countless personal stories and practical professional tips, Nesloney and Welcome not only share how they've worked to make teaching and learning better on their own campuses, they've also created a professional resource that reminds us why being a champion for our students, each and every day, is our most important job: because, above all else, #kidsdeserveit."

Jennifer LaGarde, @JenniferLaGarde, lead school library media coordinator/digital teaching and learning specialist for New Hanover County Schools in Wilmington, NC

"*Kids Deserve It!* is an inspired, concise book filled with actionable takeaways to fuel educators at every level. Whether you are a parent, teacher, or administrator, this powerful little collection of ideas and stories will nurture your spirit and refresh your memory about why you chose to work with kids in the first place. Sit back and let Adam and Todd take you on a journey to remind you of the heroism of what you do. I am inspired by the impact they have made in amplifying their message to scale through social media. Their connection to kids, their insight, and their enthusiasm continue to inspire. And without question, #kidsdeserveit."

Erik Wahl, @ErikWahl, artist, author, ambassador for kids

"In *Kids Deserve It!*, Todd and Adam offer clear and powerful strategies for educators and leaders to become innovative and creative. We can no longer afford to be tiny sparks for our children. We all must come out of our comfort zones and move into the learning zone. We must connect to other innovators. After reading this book, you will be crazy about all kids. They deserve it!"

Salome Thomas-EL, @Principal_EL, award-winning principal and author of The Immortality of Influence

"*Kids Deserve It!* is an awesome testimony to the IMPACT of educators who are willing to not only take chances in their classrooms, but also venture outside of their comfort zones to stay relevant to their students! Todd and Adam beautifully illustrate how the rewards of 'going out on a limb' definitely outweigh the risks. MUST READ for all educators!"

Daisy Dyer Duerr, @DaisyDyerDuerr, NASSP Digital Principal, Redesigning Rural Education founder, education speaker, and consultant

"*Kids Deserve It!* cuts through the clutter and gets to the heart of what matters most in education: relationships. Todd and Adam provide real, actionable stories about struggles they've faced in their combined two decades of educating kids from an array of socioeconomic backgrounds. This book comes as the role of technology is reaching increasing importance within the world of education. It's a reminder that it's not just the technology that will help kids thrive, but the people behind it."

Brett Kopf, @BrettKopf, co-founder and CEO of Remind

"*Kids Deserve It!* is a book for teachers who need inspiration to step out of their comfort zones to reach the kind of exciting learning that should take place in schools. Why? Our students do deserve that we show them learning is meaningful, and this book provides the motivation, stories, and steps to transform our classrooms."

Shelly Sanchez Terrell, @ShellTerrell, teacher trainer
and author of **The 30 Goals Challenge for Teachers**

"Education is a field where we must innovate to survive, where we have to push boundaries and do something different, where relationships are key. Todd and Adam take those ideas and put them into one place. *Kids Deserve It!* is that place. Good is no longer good enough; our kids deserve more."

Todd Whitaker, @ToddWhitaker, speaker and
author of **What Great Educators Do Differently**

"This is more than a book. Reading *Kids Deserve It!* felt more like I was having coffee with two great friends; we laughed together...we even cried a couple of times... and when the book was over, I felt inspired to change the world for kids.

Adam Welcome and Todd Nesloney have shown me what it feels like to hold inspiration in my hands. That inspiration is their new book, *Kids Deserve It!* I dare you to read it and NOT feel empowered to do something awesome for kids."

Brad Gustafson, @GustafsonBrad, Minnesota's 2016 National
Distinguished Principal, and author of **Renegade Leadership**

"Reading *Kids Deserve It!* brought tears to my eyes. It's exactly the book that students and parents wish their teachers would read and implement in school. After each chapter (e.g., 'Don't live on an Island' and 'Choices and Decisions') there are challenging questions to help the reader reflect more deeply as well as real, hands-on ideas to spark creativity and support connecting and caring.

"Especially useful are suggestions on how to find 'your people' online and tap into the power of living in the connected world. This empowers the reader to reach out and learn new professional skills and become part of a creative community of educators. A community focused less on 'getting by' and taking the easy way, and more on #imaginingwhatyoucando to change lives and to help kids—and those who love them—become part of the global community of learning."

Jack Andraka, @JackAndraka, inventor, student,
Jefferson Award winner, **National Geographic** *explorer*

"In *Kids Deserve It!*, Todd and Adam weave a series of evocative, real-life stories through a tapestry of well-thought-out and heartfelt advice. The result is a thoughtful formula for putting students at the center of our education universe. Be bold, be brave, model, innovate, connect, embrace uncertainty and discomfort, and continually learn and evolve. It's an outstanding read for educators at any level."

Angela Maiers, @AngelaMaiers, educator,
author, speaker, founder of Choose2Matter

"Slam Dunk! Nesloney and Welcome have written a book that truly shifts mindsets. For too long, school has been about compliance. Nesloney and Welcome shatter this belief and take dead aim at changing the world! They believe in kids first, and as you read *Kids Deserve It!*, you'll quickly find practical, sensible ways to begin shifting your school, classroom, and—most importantly—mindset. My absolute favorite part is in chapter seven: Showcasing ways to do 'The Little Things' is often overlooked by adults. I love the practical methods of shifting to a student-centric culture!

Hands-Down...*Kids Deserve It!* will lift you up and empower you to be the change our students need."

Ben Gilpin, @BenjaminGilpin, principal at Warner Elementary
and co-author of **Redesigning Learning Spaces**

"*Kids Deserve It!* It's a simple thought that all of our students deserve the best education possible. Who can argue with that? Through their very thoughtful, practical, and common-sense approach, Adam Welcome and Todd Nesloney show not only that kids deserve it, but give readers the necessary steps to get it done."

Peter DeWitt, @PeterMDewitt, Ed.D., author/consultant,
Finding Common Ground *blog (Education Week)*

"Todd Nesloney and Adam Welcome provide, through powerful stories, a compelling narrative that articulates how we must go above and beyond for all students. Their passion and creativity in the examples they provide will help to develop a can-do mindset for needed changes now."

Eric Sheninger, @E_Sheninger, senior fellow,
International Center for Leadership in Education

"While we all believe in kids, Adam and Todd provide inspiration and practical suggestions for how you can be a hero to kids. This books helps us to remember what we love about teaching and how to lift kids up.

My best day is when students have an awesome day. Adam and Todd provide fun and inspirational stories along with practical tips for how you can contribute to a student's best day."

Alice Keeler, @AliceKeeler, author, educational technology
specialist, coach/consultant, adjunct faculty

"Todd Nesloney and Adam Welcome not only recognize the importance of keeping children at the center of educational practice, but also provide practical tips and points of reflection that are bound to lead any school leader to personal and professional growth."

Gail Connelly, executive director,
National Association of Elementary School Principals

Pushing Boundaries and

Challenging

Conventional Thinking

TODD NESLONEY AND ADAM WELCOME

Kids Deserve It!

©2016 by Todd Nesloney and Adam Welcome

This book is available at special discounts when purchased in quantity for use as premiums, promotions, fundraising, and educational use. For inquiries and details, contact us: shelley@daveburgessconsulting.com.

Published by Dave Burgess Consulting, Inc.
San Diego, CA
http://daveburgessconsulting.com

Cover Design by Genesis Kohler
Editing and Interior Design by My Writers' Connection

Library of Congress Number: 2016939852
Paperback ISBN: 978-0-9969895-2-7
E-book ISBN: 978-0-9969895-3-4

First Printing: May 2016

Contents

Dedication

This book is dedicated to those educators who've been told they can't or they shouldn't. To those educators who have felt alone in fighting to do what's best for kids. And to those kids who've never had those educators who were willing to fight for them.

Our hope is that this book will start a spark that leads to positive and continued change.

Introduction

Money isn't what draws people to a career in education. People choose education because they want to make a difference—to change lives and impart wisdom to future generations.

Kids Deserve It! was born from a conversation two of those people (educators who wanted more for kids), two administrators who had a passion for children, education, innovation, and creativity. Both of us still remember sitting in the crowd at the National Association of Elementary School Principals Conference in 2015, listening to Erik Wahl talk about education, creativity, and imagination. From Erik's talk, we knew we wanted to create a space where we could push conventional thinking, challenge the status quo, and eliminate excuses. We wanted to be *brave*.

Both of us are principals at elementary campuses. We work with students from all walks of life. One of us works with a low-income (close to 90 percent are on a free and reduced lunch), diverse student body in a tiny rural town. The other works in a school that's part of a much larger district where the demands and struggles are something totally different, but still present.

As educators, it's easy to get caught up in what others tell us we have to complete. We quickly get beaten down by a "system" or stuck in an "it's always been this way" rut. Throughout *Kids Deserve It!*, we hope to encourage and challenge you to get unstuck and break out of that rut. Our goal is that our stories will give you hope and inspire you to persevere. We want the ideas and tools we share—resources we've used in our own careers—to help you continue to grow into your best self. Why? Because we want what's best for kids.

Our dream is for *Kids Deserve It!* to be a space where we can share our belief that growing every part of a child is truly what's best for education. As educators and adults, we must remember our sense of childlike wonder, the immense human need to be valued and noticed, and our ability to be creatively inspired and, in turn, inspire others.

Educators can't get complacent. We can't allow ourselves to be stopped by the roadblocks that will pop up in our way. We must persevere. We must keep pushing the envelope and fighting the fight to give our students the best possible education. Because each and every one of our kids deserve it.

1 Go Big, Be Creative!

What would happen if a teacher or principal came up with an idea, grabbed their students and—*boom*—tried something new? Just like that—without any fear of failure.

Or the flip side: A student comes to school with an awesome idea, and the teacher or principal runs with it. Just like that!

Why doesn't that happen? Isn't this what Common Core means by "collaboration and communication"?! Isn't this connecting and inspiring on a personal and spontaneous level?

Learning doesn't always have to be planned or prepared. It shouldn't be restricted just to the classroom, either. And it certainly doesn't stop once kids leave for the day! So many opportunities exist for learning to happen in randomly inspired moments.

The question is: Will you take the leap? Will you embrace some of those random moments to inspire learning? *But I'm not creative*, you say. Good news! We aren't born with creativity; it's something which has to be worked at, practiced, and developed.

Imagine the environment your students could walk into daily—one where they never knew what exciting thing was going to take place because creativity ruled in your classroom. They learned from you that

---

Will you take the leap? Will you embrace some of those random moments to inspire learning?

---

imagination ignites ideas—and their ideas are just as valued as those of adults. What if we dedicated time each day to explore new ideas and took off our kids' training wheels to see how far they could go?!

Give Them Something to Talk About

Shortly after I (Todd) visited the Ron Clark Academy in Atlanta, Georgia, I transformed my classroom. Few experiences in my career have compared to the impact of that visit. Watching teachers like Ron Clark and Kim Bearden forever shaped how I think about creativity and emotional experiences in the classroom.

Kim talked about building emotional experiences into what we do in the classroom and stressed how we have to be excited, spontaneous, and whimsical. She shared how transforming our classroom space can have a huge impact on learning. Kim is right. Research shows our memories are based on emotional experiences.

So I took Kim's advice. I returned to Texas with a new idea. After a couple of weeks of planning and spending about $35 at Dollar Tree on supplies, the "Nez Hospital" was born.

For a week before the transformation, I built up anticipation. I told the kids every day they did *not* want to miss school on Friday. It would be unlike anything they'd ever experienced. That's all I told them. They had no idea what was coming, but boy, were they intrigued!

The Thursday evening before the "Don't Miss" Friday, I transformed my classroom into an operating room. I covered the walls in clear plastic tablecloths, put blue tablecloths on all the desks, displayed a 3D graphic of a beating heart on my projector, downloaded the sound of a beating heart to play on my iPod, and prepared several activities using gummy worms, red dyed water, tweezers, gallon baggies, and more.

When the kids arrived the following day, they were met by a locked classroom door with a sign stating, "The Doctor will be with you momentarily." Precisely when the bell rang, I burst out of my classroom, dressed as a doctor wearing glasses (which I never do) and a substitute pass to wear with the name "Dr. Nezbit" on it. I greeted the students with a huge welcome and a new accent. I introduced myself as Dr. Nezbit and explained their teacher was out today, and I would be taking them through a New Doctor Training Program, sponsored by the Nez Hospital.

As kids entered the "operating room," they put on their "surgical attire" (masks, gloves, eye goggles, hair nets, and science lab aprons that I had borrowed from the high school chemistry department).

Throughout the class I told stories, and the kids completed experiment after experiment tailored to the standards we were learning at the time. We did everything from using gummy worms (parasites) and red dyed water (blood) to measure the length of the parasites in the water, to creating a cafeteria space that fit the most people while having designs for three different cafeteria tables, to using math problems to solve hospital inconsistencies in patient records. The experience was truly magical.

As I ate lunch with the students, the principal walked over and said, "Dr. Nezbit, is everything going okay today?" After she walked away, one kid said, "She does know you're not really Dr. Nezbit, right?" *Classic!*

I told the students when Mr. Nesloney returned on Monday, he would have certificates for every student who graduated from the New Doctor Training Program. Let's just say the weekend got away from me, and I totally forgot to make the certificates. Students were lined up at my door Monday morning, ready to tell me ALL about their day with Dr. Nezbit, and asking where their certificates were. I spent my conference period making certificates! I had to ensure every child got one, otherwise I don't think they would've allowed me to leave at the end of the day!

From then on, students asked when Dr. Nezbit was returning. That day happened several years ago, and students are *still* talking about it.

I could have been too scared to try something new. I could have made excuses about why it wouldn't work, how my students couldn't handle it, why my principal wouldn't allow it, or why I didn't have time for it. But I pushed the excuses aside, stepped out of my comfort zone, and ran with an idea. And I couldn't be happier. This experience truly transformed me as an educator.

Go Out on a Limb

Isn't this the way the modern workforce is? Do any of us go to jobs where nothing spontaneous ever happens? As educators, our jobs never follow a script. Even days that are well-planned are filled with unexpected happenings, little blessings, and even some trials and triumphs.

We believe that educators have a responsibility to build an environment of excitement, creativity, and value. We can't be afraid to go out on a limb and try something new. Yes, sometimes the limb might break and we'll have to grab hold of another to keep from crashing. But maybe it *won't* break. Maybe we'll be able to climb even higher and create something totally new that heightens the imaginations of students throughout both the classroom and the school. When that happens, you'll know your kids are on the path to using their creative thinking, curiosity, and discovery skills—skills they will use long after they leave your classroom.

Kids Deserve It is about stepping out on that limb even if it might break—doing something unexplored and unexpected. You *can* bring that fire to your classroom! Our schools deserve it, our communities deserve it, and our kids deserve it!

Even days that are well-planned are filled with unexpected happenings.

Things to Consider and Tweet

1. How can you "go big"?
2. What's a new way to be creative in class to increase your students' excitement?
3. Don't be afraid to chart new waters and take a risk. What's an idea you've wanted to try but haven't?

#KidsDeserveIt

2 Don't Live on an Island

Education is very different today than when we started teaching. We taught only within the four walls of our classroom. We never even imagined speaking to—much less collaborating with—others from around the world. We were focused; heads down, nose to the grindstone. And in the process, we learned that teaching can become a very lonely profession.

Worse than loneliness is the negativity that comes when we're in an environment where, even if you want to innovate and push boundaries, you feel isolated by people who aren't willing to do anything but push back. In order to do what you know is best for kids, you may begin to feel like you have to teach behind a closed door and keep your head down. That's not thriving; it's barely surviving. And that kind of repetitive, secluded existence is certainly *not* conducive to new ideas.

Whatever the reason for the isolation, if you want to create that spark, you have to "get off the island" and start collaborating. The good news is that you can choose whom to connect and collaborate with—and they don't have to be within the walls of your building.

Yes, it's scary to step outside our comfort zones, reach out to others for help, or share our own ideas. But every day, we tell our students to try and learn new things—to be *brave*. How can we as educators not model the same behavior?

Similarly, we can no longer say we don't understand something the "kids are all talking about." Do a Google or YouTube search. The knowledge is at our fingertips. We live in a world where we can no longer claim ignorance—only an unwillingness to learn.

While you may think we're talking about being "techie," what we're actually talking about is being *relevant* for your kids. Today's students are surrounded by technology and information. They aren't growing

We live in a world where we can no longer claim ignorance—only an unwillingness to learn.

up in the same world we lived in when we were in school. We have to understand that technology, YouTube, and social media are part of today's world, and it's our job to prepare them to handle it.

And if you're tempted to respond by saying you're too busy to get connected, we think it's only fair to tell you we firmly believe we all have time for *exactly* what we choose to have time for. If you say you don't have time to get connected, you're actually saying that other things in your life are more important.

Let's stop making excuses. Your fellow teachers deserve for you to be connected. Your students deserve it. Your community deserves it. *You* deserve it. You'll be a stronger educator because of being connected. We don't really have a choice anymore. If we're truly concerned with doing what is best for kids, we must get out of our isolation and connect with others—in and out of our profession. Our kids deserve it!

Things to Consider and Tweet

1. Do you feel like you're on an island? How could talking with other administrators via Voxer or Twitter create an amazing lifeline throughout the day?
2. How can we encourage more educators to connect outside their four walls?
3. What was your biggest fear when you first reached out to someone online? What did you gain from reaching out? Did that make it less scary?
4. How can telling others how you got connected help them believe they can do the same?

#KidsDeserveIt

3 Innovate! Be Different!

Educators work in a field steeped in tradition. Schools are filled with practices we've been doing for decades, and many days we wonder why we're doing so many things the way we've always done them. (We find it funny to hear people talk about "twenty-first-century" skills. Did we use twentieth-century skills?)

Sure, traditions can be an important part of our schools' cultures, but when it comes to learning, using decades-old tactics won't cut it. We can't expect our kids to be growing, learning, and pushing boundaries unless we're doing the same. How dare we ask our students to show up every day and learn if we're not learning and pushing ourselves?

The use of technology and collaboration skills should be expected and practiced daily in every educational organization—from the administration to the teachers to the students. We must lead by example. If you want your teachers or students to integrate technology, don't walk around your school writing notes on a yellow legal pad. Grab a tablet and digitize your life! Show people you value the tools kids are using.

We must continually find ways to innovate our practices. We have to step out of our comfort zones, take risks, and be brave. Push the envelope—make a mistake. You'll be stronger and more innovative for your kids. They don't have the time to wait on us. When we drag our feet, fearful about testing new technology in the classroom, we're wasting prime learning opportunities.

Creativity is another skill that we must hone if we want our students to learn that sharing their own creative ideas is a risk worth taking. So many educators tell us, "I'm not creative." As if creativity is a skill you either have or you don't. That's a myth! Artist and business strategist Erik Wahl and education speaker and author Dave Burgess, both of whom we greatly admire, talk extensively about creativity, and stress that it isn't something you're born with. Rather, creativity is a learned skill that you develop by working at it—continually.

Both of us have experienced moments of amazing creativity, but they didn't come easily. They came through trial and error, mistake after mistake, and as the result of many conversations with people who pushed our thinking and helped us grow. We call these people "thinking partners," and they are so important to cultivating creativity. We

Creativity is a learned skill that you develop by working at it—continually.

constantly text, vox, and Tweet our ideas to each other. In school, we pair our students with reading and writing partners for the same reason that we seek out thinking partners: We need people to propel us!

If you don't currently have a thinking partner, find one! How could you locate one? If you do have one, who is it, and how does he inspire you to innovate? Do you have a "place" to converse with your thinking partner? There really are many options! Join a Twitter chat, jump into an education Facebook group, search out blogs, or even start a conversation with someone new in the teacher's lounge or across the hall.

Don't let the excuse, "I'm not creative," stop you from trying new things. *Everyone* is creative. You must access the genius inside you. You deserve it. Your colleagues deserve it. Kids deserve it.

Do Something New! (Ask for Help!)

Before I (Todd) was hired to be the Principal/Lead Learner at Navasota Intermediate School in 2014, I received a Twitter direct message asking if I liked teaching in a project-based learning (PBL) classroom, which I was doing at the time. Subsequently, I was asked if I'd want to teach at a PBL school and, finally, would I consider *leading* a PBL-based school? I was intrigued, but thought I wasn't ready to leave the classroom.

After many conversations and a few interviews with Navasota ISD, I was hired and tasked with the challenge of taking over a reconstituted school. When a school struggles with test scores for three consecutive years, the state of Texas steps in to provide guidance on how to "fix" the issue. At Navasota Intermediate, the decision was made to start over with completely new staff, while giving all former employees there the opportunity to reapply if interested. Essentially, I inherited a campus with no staff and had to hire personnel for all thirty-eight positions at the school in a matter of months.

I interviewed more than 150 applicants face-to-face, over the phone, and through Skype and Google Hangout. (See how using technology can make life a little easier?) It was an exciting time, and just a little terrifying. I hoped to put together just the right team. As the summer started, I knew I needed to find a way to bring my new staff together and encourage and challenge them to stretch and connect—even before we arrived on campus a couple months later. So I launched a

Summer Learning Series (or #SummerLS), and each week I gave my new staff a challenge they could complete to enhance their practice.

The first challenge was to create a Twitter account. I recorded a how-to video and posted it on my YouTube channel. I sent the link with some explanation of the challenge to my new staff. I'd forgotten people other than my staff members follow my YouTube channel, and over the next few days, I received emails from a couple of random educators who saw the video and really liked it. Several asked if they could participate with my staff! Why not? So I created a public blog space where anyone could join in.

I then decided that if I was going to encourage my staff to connect with and learn from others, I should reach out to my professional learning network (PLN)—people I'd connected with online and through conferences—and ask them to help me with my weekly challenges. Over the next couple of months, along with my PLN, I created challenge after challenge for educators to complete.

Thanks to Angela Maiers, Erin Klein, Eric Sheninger, Amber Teamann, Tom Murray, Stacey Huffine, Chris Kesler, Dave Burgess, and so many more, the #SummerLS was a huge success. By the end of the summer we had more than three thousand educators from eight different countries participating. Later in the year, we won an EduBlog Award for Best Open Professional Development.

Organizing a Summer Learning Series was new for me—something I'd never even thought I could create. But by taking the risk to try something new and reaching out to a few friends for help, my staff grew from it—and so did I!

Months later, I furthered the challenges through an Educator Learning Series (#EduLS). While neither #SummerLS nor #EduLS are still running live, you can find all the challenges at summerls2014.blogspot.com and educatorlearningseries.blogspot.com, respectively. Educators continue to tell me they came across the blogs and gained learning experiences! Who would have thought my idea to get my new staff connected would impact thousands across the globe?

Get a Different Viewpoint

At the beginning of last year, our school Twitter account had over seven hundred followers, and I (Adam) had Tweeted more than thirteen thousand times in the previous three years. Every teacher on campus was actively sharing their classrooms' stories on Twitter, and parents Tweeted back constantly. It was amazing! But something was missing. While sitting in a fifth-grade classroom, it hit me. We really needed to share the voice of our students. We needed them to be a part of the conversation, and not just a silent voice. How do they view our school? Students needed to be Tweeting as well!

Immediately I texted my idea to two fifth-grade parents: "I want students to start Tweeting at school and your child would be perfect. Are you in?"

Their replies came within three minutes: "Sounds awesome!" "Go!"

I gave the kids an iPad and sent them to take photos around campus. Then we crafted Tweets, talked about hashtags, acceptable messages to share with our community, privacy, and much more. All the students' Tweets went through our school account, tagged #KidTweet. After a few days under my tutelage, they had free rein to take photos and compose Tweets together throughout the day. Such amazing collaboration!

You can give kids a handout to read, a movie to watch, or a lecture to listen to. But a hands-on approach with social media is so much more effective! Tweeting let them feel what it was like to share with the world. They were learning how to interact with our school community and loving every minute! They even added all their photos to our Flickr account and created a great archive for the year.

Within a few hours of their first Tweet, I was accosted with, "I want to be an intern, Mr. Welcome!" Lots of other kids approached me, eager to be involved and share their voices as well. Instantly, our school's social media intern program was born! Sully and Callie trained the next interns, and afterward, each new set of interns trained the following set. The students' awesome teamwork gave our community a new glimpse at school life—the kids' viewpoint! I loved seeing their Tweets pop up on my phone. The students loved this program—and so did the adults!

A few weeks after we started the intern program, our local Rotary Club heard about it and asked the kids and me to present about social media. Of course I went to their meeting, but the students did all the talking—it was their story to share!

The Risks and Rewards of Innovation

Getting connected online and learning how to use social media effectively is essential—for us *and* our students. Digital tools, like YouTube and Twitter, can open the door to new information, creative ideas, and all sorts of amazing opportunities. But social media also opens the door for mistakes. (Like shooting off a Tweet when you're angry. Don't do it!) Social media isn't going away. In fact, it's only going to become more a part of our daily lives. That's why we must be our kids' social media guides, showing them the appropriate path to follow. Twitter is a mainstream communication tool (used by NBA players, members of the United Nations, the Dalai Lama—even the Pope!). More importantly to our students, colleges and employers check applicants' Twitter and Facebook profiles. We must teach our kids how to use these tools—and to use them wisely.

The ideas we've shared here only scratch the surface of the innovative learning experiences that educators are doing. For example, Ryan McLane has led a *Teach Like a Pirate* day for his entire student population, where the teachers teach interactive lessons about topics they're passionate about, and students get to pick which classes they want to attend. Brad Gustafson uses drones, augmented reality, green screens, lunch DJs, and more to enhance the learning environment for his students.

But be warned: Thinking differently comes with some risk. We can share our ideas and challenge you to be creative, but we don't want to sugarcoat reality. When you choose to innovate and be unique, you will experience some failure. And sometimes it stings more than you'd

---

We must teach our kids how to use these tools— and to use them wisely.

---

like.

Both of us have watched what we thought were our greatest lesson ideas go up in flames. And then we've had to face the eyes. You know—*those* eyes. The ones staring with the "I-always-knew-that-wouldn't-work" look. Frankly, we see the "alien" look as a badge of honor because we only get it when we're pushing the envelope and moving forward!

Or maybe you want to innovate, but at every turn, someone is telling you that you can't. Or you're not allowed. Or the students can't handle it. Or there aren't enough resources. Some days it's hard to pick yourself up from the failures, the stares, and the negative comments. Sometimes you just want to crawl into a hole and never innovate again. We know. We've been there. But we must stop listening to the naysayers. We can't let them control or limit our creativity and innovation! Don't accept "no," especially when it's accompanied by, "This is the way we've always done things." "No" isn't fair to the kids, teachers, parents, or your colleagues who need your fresh, imaginative ideas!

The good news is that the old adage is true: "With great risk comes great reward." If we're willing to stick out our necks, stumble and fall, and occasionally get hurt, we'll end up giving our students a better education than they ever dreamed of.

When you read stories about those who pushed limits—Gandhi, Mother Teresa, Einstein, Thomas Edison—they weren't always supported or believed in by others, either. They faced backlash, doubters, and pessimists. Thankfully, they chose to ignore the naysayers and became significant difference-makers in history.

You have the same choice every day. You can choose what's always been done—the safe and easy. Or, you can choose what's less simple, potentially more difficult, and absolutely more rewarding. While you're

People don't instigate great change or significantly impact others' lives by choosing the familiar path.

considering your options, think about this: People don't instigate great change or significantly impact others' lives by choosing the familiar path. If you want to be remembered, choose to be different—and be remembered for the impact your choice makes on your students. Dare to take the risks necessary to inspire kids to see their limitless potential and push their own envelopes one day. Innovating doesn't always end perfectly. Things don't always work out as planned. But we learn the most through our failures. As long as we are trying new ideas, pushing ourselves outside of our comfort zones, and learning from our mistakes, we will improve. And when we improve, our practice improves, and ultimately, our students improve! We've got to continually push ourselves, grow, innovate, and find ways to be different! The kids deserve it!

Things to Consider and Tweet

1. What is the biggest fear holding you back from innovating?
2. When is the last time you stepped outside your comfort zone and tried something new? How did it turn out?
3. How are you encouraging your students to innovate and be different? Your peers? Your leaders?
4. How are you encouraging student voice?

#KidsDeserveIt

4 Never Slam the Door

Every educator has had *that student*—the one who pushes all the right (or wrong!) buttons. The one who works to make himself seem unlovable. But if you've been an educator for any length of time, you know when you finally reach *that student*, his life is changed—and so is yours.

As teachers, we dealt with a few of these students, and as administrators, we see even more. Every day, we come into contact with child after child who is hurting deeply. These children act out because they're academically behind, want attention, or they don't know how to act differently because of how they've been raised.

What do you do with these students? How do you even begin to reach them or handle them? Take away recess? Make them walk laps? Put them in detention? No. Kids deserve to know they're cared about—unconditionally—on a deep level. They need to know you see them as more than a name in a grade book or a warm body in a chair. They need to know you're willing to put in the time and effort to build a relationship with them. You never know when those students might turn a corner. When they might start to trust. When they might start to lower their walls and allow you to see what's really going on in their world. And when they do, you reap huge dividends!

When we approach discipline, we start by sitting down and having a conversation with the student. Many times adults want to resort to punishment or yelling, but when a child acts out, they're often doing so from a place of pain or hurt. Often, they just want someone to listen. They need to feel heard and have someone support them. But too often, rather than getting the support they need, those students endure even more pain when exasperated adults slam doors in their faces—figuratively and, unfortunately, sometimes literally—and affirm their belief that no one cares.

So what does support look like? Sometimes, it means sitting on the floor with a student who is hiding under his desk, or walking down the hall with her so she can have a few minutes to cool off. Sometimes, it means going outside and shooting a few hoops with a student or simply sitting with him in our office and talking.

When we talk to students, we start with listening. We let them speak. We try to understand what they're feeling. Why did they act out? Why are they upset? What we hear from them helps us form a plan *with* the students to make sure unacceptable behavior isn't repeated.

When you listen to a child, you give him back his voice, and you're able to delve much deeper into the root of the problem. You're also able to figure out a solution and set goals together, rather than handing down punishment that addresses the symptom rather than the cause.

When you listen to a child, you give him back his voice.

Let Kids Know You Care About Them

Three years ago, one student took *a lot* of my (Adam) time. Usually, the reason for his visit to my office wasn't something terrible; it was disruptive. Almost every day, I talked with this student—at recess, in my office—or with his mom over the phone.

My approach to discipline is to talk and talk and talk with kids. How did they misbehave? Why did they misbehave? What are the next steps to keep them from repeating the behavior? I then check in with them constantly—sometimes as many as three to five times a day.

After a few meetings with this student's parents, I decided to do a home visit—something I've done ever since I was a teacher. I coordinate with the parents, but it's always a surprise for the kids when I show up. The first place I want kids to show me during a home visit is their room. If their bed isn't made, we make it. If the room is dirty, we clean it!

When I arrived at this student's house, as usual, I was met with big, surprised eyes! After he showed me the chickens and tree forts in the back yard, he asked the question:

"Why are you here, Mr. Welcome?"

"Because I care about you!" I said. "And I want to help you with your decisions at school. I know you can do better."

He got it. The very next day things started to change. The boy's parents thanked me for coming over and spending time with their family, something, they said, no teacher or administrator had done before.

That was two years ago. The student is now in fifth grade, and his energy, behavior, work output, and overall attitude have improved immensely. The past two years weren't perfect—we've had some hiccups—but we've also had some big improvements along the way.

During the final week of school last year, I called this student to my office. As soon as we sat down, he said:

"I didn't do anything, Mr. Welcome."

To which I replied, "Yes, you have. You've matured! You've improved your decision-making! You're doing your best in class. You've made more friends. You're happy. You smile more. You're a team player. *I. Am. So. Proud. Of. You.*"

We both started crying a little, and then the student gave me a hug! When I called the student's mom to tell her what happened, *she* started crying!

Your Kids Need You

We have to view every child as a seed waiting to bloom. We may be the teacher who plants the seed, we may be the one to water it, or we may be the one who actually gets to watch it grow. As elementary educators, we often don't get to see the fruits of our labor until long down the road, but a lack of immediate payoff doesn't mean we stop investing time in our students. It's so important to remember that you're creating the right conditions for them to take root and grow up to be the best versions of themselves.

Students will frustrate you and take an exorbitant amount of your time. But there's a reason for this: They need you. They need you to trust them, accept them, and care for them. And you always have the choice to show them you care. In fact, sometimes we can invest in students and show them how much they mean to us even before we've met them.

Your Belief Can Make All the Difference

A few years ago, I (Todd) read a story Angela Maiers shared about Arin Kress, a fifth-grade science and social studies teacher. Arin wrote and mailed a letter to every one of her incoming students before she ever met them. She told them she already cared deeply for them and believed in them. She explained that every student was getting a fresh new start, and that they were going to work together to find each one's unique version of success.

I was so impacted by Arin's story that I decided to do the same with my students. Before school started, I wrote a letter to each of my seventy-five incoming fifth graders, letting them know how much I cared about them even though I'd never met them. I also told them we would work together to help them find *their* version of success.

I sent the letters before "Meet the Teacher" night, and while a few parents acknowledged that the letters had arrived, none of the students said a word about them.

At the end of the school year, one parent came to me with a letter her son had written because he wanted to tell me something. Her son was a special education student who struggled in my class.

As she and I read the letter together, we both cried. Her son told me as long as he could remember, he'd been classified as a "special education student," and his teachers had always treated him differently. But during the summer, before he became part of my class or even met me, he got my letter.

He said no one had ever told him they believed in him before they'd even met him. Never before had a teacher told him he could be successful outside of the help he'd receive in his special education world. Before his fifth-grade year, he had never passed any state standardized exam. In fact, he felt like he'd never found any success. But this particular year, he passed all of his state standardized exams. He believed the only reason for his improvement was that someone believed in him before they even met him.

How powerful is that? I still tear up when I talk about this. Kids want to know they matter to you. They want to know you see them, hear them, and believe in them—unconditionally.

This little boy forever touched my heart and reminded me sometimes our smallest actions make the biggest difference—even though we may not see the results for months or years to come.

Kids want to know they matter to you.

You *Are* Making an Impact

Seeing the changes that occur in students when they know you truly care about them is an amazing feeling—one that reminds you why you became a teacher in the first place. When those walls come down or you see new light in a child's eyes, you'll know you're making a difference.

Please, *never* slam the door on a child. Never give up on a student, no matter how hard it is or how many times you wonder how you can reach the child. We have to remember our students deserve our belief in them. We may be the only person who can reach them—the only person who will even try. Truth is, we may never know the difference you're making in a child's life, but believe this: You *are* making an impact.

What can you do? Open your arms and doors wide. Invite them in. Listen, show empathy, and build relationships with them. And never close the door. Your kids deserve it.

Things to Consider and Tweet

1. Who is your most memorable *that student*? Who is your *that student* this year?
2. What are some ways you've built deeper relationships and connected with kids?
3. How has your life been impacted by children who are the hardest to love?

#KidsDeserveIt

5 Make That Phone Call

There's power in a simple phone call. We've seen the positive impact a phone call can have on our students, and we've experienced the power personally. You see, Ron Clark (yes, Disney Teacher of the Year, founder of The Ron Clark Academy, *that* Ron Clark) telephoned us—both of us—on the same day.

It Started as a Joke

Todd and I were talking on Voxer one morning about different challenges we were going through as principals. Honestly, Todd was being pretty dramatic about one thing or another—he tends to get that way. I decided to call his school office and play a little joke. When his office manager answered, I told her I was Ron Clark calling for Mr. Nesloney. I had just seen him on Persicope surprising a school in Tennessee. So I decided I'd call Todd, pretend to be Ron Clark, and see what happened.

Just Kidding—or Not!

Adam knows how much I admire Ron Clark. He also knew I had recently had dinner with Kim Bearden, co-founder of the Ron Clark Academy. I had just returned to my office that afternoon from a training when my phone rang. I answered it and heard my office manager say, "It's Ron Clark."

It took a few seconds for the feeling of stunned disbelief to subside. *Ron Clark? Seriously?*

She asked if she could patch him through. *Of course!* The next thing I knew, "Ron Clark" was talking to me, asking if I was at school, and telling me he was about to pull up in his big red bus and surprise my staff! I was on the verge of shock when I heard the next few words: "Just kidding! It's me—Adam." Yeah, Adam punked me. And punked me good!

So what did I do? I Tweeted about it, of course, and made sure to tag the real Ron Clark. Right away, Ron Clark favorited the Tweet *and responded*. Ironic and funny, the first thing he told me was he had tried to call my school three different times, but no one had answered. I was sure he was joking, of course, until he sent a second Tweet assuring me he was serious.

The next thing I knew, my phone rang again, and this time it *was* Ron Clark—the real Ron Clark. My educational hero—someone I'd looked up to since I was a junior in high school—was talking to *me* on the phone like we were old buddies. We chatted for about fifteen minutes before he asked me for Adam's mobile phone number so he could tell him not to mess with his buddy, Todd Nesloney. Epic.

One Simple, Amazing Phone Call

After my prank call to Todd, I went back to work. I was writing some ideas in Evernote while reading the hilarious Twitter exchange between Ron and Todd when my cell phone rang. The call was from Georgia—where the Ron Clark Academy is located.

No way. Ron Clark was now calling *me*! We chatted for fifteen minutes about education, kids, and how much we love our work. It was just a simple phone call—and it was *amazing*. When we said goodbye, I was filled with inspiration and energy. Thank you, Ron Clark!

Why do we share this story? Because there's power in a single phone call. We have the ability to brighten a day or fill a heart with hope simply by picking up the phone. The power of a phone call is real, profound, and important because voice connects people in a way email does not.

Hats Off to You

I (Todd) started "Hats Off to You" cards this year. My school has children who come from difficult backgrounds and discipline can become an issue very quickly. We were about a month into school, but already felt beaten down by the amount of discipline issues we were dealing with. After some honest conversations among campus staff, we realized we were putting all of our focus on the students making incorrect choices, instead of putting equal focus on those making good choices.

"Hats Off to You" was born as an effort to change this. Each week, every staff member gets eight little encouragement cards to hand out to kids they see making great choices! When a student receives a card, he gets to come to the office while an administrator calls his parents to share why their child is being celebrated and to tell the parents how proud we are of their child. The next morning, all the "Hats Off" card recipients are announced to the school, and at the end of the week, twenty randomly selected "Hats Off" card recipients get to go outside to play a game with the principal.

"Hats Off" has changed everything. Discipline issues dropped by half—yes, *half*—within three days! And we don't just see the "always behaving" kids in the office with the "Hats Off" cards. Even students who sometimes make poor choices have received them and been celebrated for their good choices.

And the best part? The phone calls! We had kids cry, parents cry, and yes, sometimes we cry along with them. The simple act of calling a parent to celebrate his or her child costs you nothing. But to the families who don't often hear—especially from school administrators—about how great their children are, these phone calls mean so much.

Catch Them Doing Something Great

The other day, I (Adam) was hanging out in a fifth-grade classroom where the students were working on maps of our downtown. One student in particular was so juiced to show me his work; he excitedly explained all the different details, landmarks, and creative additions he had made.

Suddenly, he grabbed his school-assigned iPad, logged into Google Apps, and showed me his writing piece which went along with his map. I asked him why he hadn't shared this with me yet via Google, and he did so immediately.

This student blew me away with his work, and I knew what I needed to do: I needed to call his home and praise him to his parents.

One of my favorite pastimes as principal is to hang out in a class, notice students doing something totally amazing, and then call their parents on my cell phone. So I took this student outside the classroom, with his iPad, and told him we were calling his mom. It was awesome!

He gave me her mobile number, and we dialed her up on speaker-phone. Like most parents, she was a little hesitant to hear my voice—until I started to explain. And then she started crying, telling him how proud she was of his work, of him as a son, and as a big brother. She thanked me profusely for calling. Did I say that was awesome? You better believe it!

You Can't Call Home Too Often

Educators are expected to do a lot. At times, the list of tasks can seem unending. But one thing neither of us would ever want to take off that list is calling parents to celebrate their children. It's one of the most important and rewarding aspects of our work. We believe it is essential to building relationships with our students and their families. And the parents we call always thank us for taking time from our busy schedules to brag on their children.

We truly believe you can't call home too often. There's such power in taking a minute to tell someone you notice them. To take time to share

---

Taking time out of your schedule to make a simple phone call can make a world of difference.

---

a laugh, ask how they're doing, tell them they did a great job—anything! Take a moment to call parents and tell them you see greatness in their child. Or take a moment to call a child at home to let him know how much you enjoy seeing his smiling face every day.

Taking time out of your schedule to make a simple phone call can make a world of difference. And you don't have to limit your calls to your students' parents. Recently, we started calling the parents and families of our *staff* when they do amazing things! No matter what our age, it's a great feeling when our parents or families can hear what great things we're doing.

We spoke to one another after talking with Ron Clark to help process our feelings of excitement, and maybe even a little awe. He may never know it, but his call made a huge difference in both of our lives. One we won't soon forget.

If we felt like that after someone we so highly respect called us, how might a parent feel after you, as a teacher or principal, call them with a positive message about their child? We'll tell you how they'll feel: They'll feel *amazing* because you took the time, showed that you cared, and that you believe their child is worthy of being celebrated.

Call home—often! Call home to celebrate kids! All kids deserve to be celebrated.

Things to Consider and Tweet

1. When was the last time you called a parent at home to celebrate his or her child? What happened?
2. Have you found time to celebrate every child? They all deserve a phone call home. Find one thing special about them and celebrate it.

#KidsDeserveIt

6 Be a Leader Worth Following

We're guessing all of us have worked with a "leader" who didn't lead—a person in a position of power who didn't steer the ship. We've both worked under amazing administrators, but we've also worked with those who screamed, went to jail, and one whom we call "He-Who-Shall-Not-Be-Named." Yes, it's safe to say we've seen all kinds!

We like the image of a ship when we think of leadership. A ship can sit on the water and float whether there's a captain aboard or not. But ships weren't designed just to sit and float. They were designed to travel. If there is no captain behind the wheel, a ship can run ashore, hit something, or go in the opposite direction of where it was headed. A ship needs a captain—someone who can take the wheel and steer it in the right direction. Every crew—be it a school or a classroom—needs a captain who *knows* how to lead. As Antoine de Saint-Exupéry stated: "If you want to build a ship, don't gather people together to collect wood and don't assign them tasks and work, but rather, teach them to long for the endless immensity of the sea."[1]

---

1 Antoine de Saint-Exupéry, *The Wisdom of the Sands*, trans. Stuart Gilbert (New York: Harcourt, Brace and Company, 1950).

Working on a campus where the leader doesn't lead—where the leader is absent, indecisive, or belligerent—is one of the hardest aspects of teaching. As principals, we believe it's important to be actively involved in classrooms. Administrative leaders need to take time to co-teach or model lessons, pull small, tutoring groups, plan with teachers, lead after-school tutoring, read with kids, serve with car, bus, and lunch duty, and so much more.

Classroom leaders need to create environments that encourage collaboration and innovation—and not just between students. Classroom leaders know how to communicate effectively. They know when to push, but they also know when to pull back. They know the importance of building relationships. Classroom leaders need to model what it looks like to take risks and to be different. Classroom leaders also know that leading doesn't always happen by standing at the front of the classroom lecturing.

Poor leaders are great at making excuses—about the amount of paperwork they have to do, or the number of interruptions they get each day, or any of the other demands on their time. Some complain that all they do is *put out fires* all day long. But we believe that if you're busy building relationships and connecting with people, the number of fires will go way down. And yes, it *is* possible to be actively involved in classrooms and still get your work done. Does it take some creative finagling? Yep, sure does! But it's worth it. When you're holed up in your captain's quarters—whether that's the teacher's desk or the principal's office—you're not leading, you're managing. Leaders need to be out on deck, watching the water, steering the ship, and encouraging the crew.

Leaders need to be out on deck, watching the water, steering the ship, and encouraging the crew.

SEVEN PRACTICES THAT WILL MAKE YOU A BETTER LEADER

1. Get a clear vision for your classroom, school, and district. Know where you want to go and then chart your course for success.

2. Be courageous enough to make the decisions that are best for your kids—and then stick to them.

3. Own up to your failures. Far too many leaders are afraid to say, "I'm sorry," or, "I made a bad call." Everyone is human—even leaders. Everyone makes mistakes. We've had to go before our teams countless times and say, "I screwed up," or, "I need to apologize for a decision I made." It isn't easy, but owning your mistakes earns your followers' respect.

4. Create environments where innovation is the norm by taking risks. Leaders need to take risks and push boundaries A) because doing so benefits the students, and B) because those you lead will follow your example. Keep in mind, though, that risk-taking also comes with a lot of failure, and that's okay! As long as we're learning from our failure.

5. Be willing to lean on others and ask for help. It's hard but necessary. Far too many people think asking for help is a sign of incompetence or weakness; it's *not*!

6. Give credit and allow others to shine. A good leader never acts like success is a direct reflection of them. Good leaders know when and how to recognize others and allow them to be the star.

7. Be a lifelong learner. Be someone who is constantly learning and growing personally while challenging and encouraging others to do the same.

A side note about personal and professional development for leaders: What message does a leader send if she isn't learning? What will teachers think if their administrators don't believe in social media or just can't "get" Tweeting or blogging about the district's story? How can leaders encourage others to be relevant if they're not staying relevant themselves? The answer is, they can't. When leaders choose not to learn, the message staff members receive is that personal growth isn't necessary; using social media or other technology tools isn't important. They'll find it difficult to get excited about using these tools or will get frustrated if they want to use the tools but don't have the support of leadership. And when teachers see administrators from neighboring districts leading from the front—pushing change, innovating with their teams, and preaching their mission and vision to all who will listen—they'll want to change schools so they, too, can be part of a growing team.

When leaders don't lead, no one grows, and superstars leave. Without strong leadership, exceptional team members will leave in search of a campus where they are challenged to grow. They'll look for a leader—not a warm body in an office. Don't allow your people to jump ship. Keep them on your team by growing with them. We must constantly be moving, growing, learning, pushing, failing, falling—and getting up stronger and smarter than we were before!

Whatever your role in your school is, commit to being a leader worth following. Don't be afraid to challenge your leaders—ask them what they're learning. Ask them to go on an adventure—to team-teach with you, or try something new alongside you!

Leaders must lead. They must take the helm and control their ships.

Be the captain and ensure your ship is doing what it was designed to do!

Whatever your role in your school is, commit to being a leader worth following.

Things to Consider and Tweet

1. How have you led alongside colleagues while pushing them to grow and learn?
2. Has your fear of admitting mistakes kept you from apologizing to your colleagues? What might you need to apologize for?
3. How have you led recently? What needs to change for you to be a better leader?

#KidsDeserveIt

7 Do the Little Things

We learn a lot from our leaders. Their examples help to shape us and our decisions. They can help us grow and consider new ideas and perspectives. Sometimes we learn new things; sometimes they simply remind us of little things we've forgotten. But those *little things* can often make the biggest difference for our students. We've shared some of our favorite "little things" below.

MAKE PEOPLE FEEL IMPORTANT

Last summer, I (Todd) had to book a last-minute hotel for one night in Austin. I wanted to find something inexpensive and decided to try a Holiday Inn Express that had recently opened. During the first day of the conference I was attending—before I had checked into the hotel—I got a call from a member of the hotel staff. She told me they were excited to have me as a guest and asked if they could do anything before I arrived to ensure I had a great stay.

I was taken aback. Never before had a hotel called me before I checked in to tell me they were excited I was staying with them, much less ask me if I needed anything prepared!

When I arrived, the staff was incredibly friendly. The doorman greeted me right away, shook my hand, and asked me how my day was. The clerk at the front desk was all smiles. And the next morning, a handwritten note had been slid under my door. It was from the hotel manager who said he hoped I had a great stay and would return again.

Wow! Aside from the notecard, these little things cost the hotel nothing, but they made a huge difference to me. I even called the manager to let him know how important his staff made me feel. Months later, I'm still telling everyone about this. And the next time I need a hotel in Austin, I guarantee I'll be staying at this Holiday Inn Express.

We can make people feel important at schools, too. We need to find ways to make our buildings and classrooms the most welcoming and encouraging places on the planet. Try some of these ideas to make people at school feel welcome:

- Send "welcome back" letters or postcards to students before school starts in the fall or after winter break.
- Play music in the classroom.
- Write thank you notes to parents and others who visit your classroom, volunteer, or donate items.
- Call students' homes just to show you care.
- Attend the extracurricular activities of your students *and* your coworkers.
- Greet everyone who walks through your door with a high five, fist bump, hug, or a warm smile.
- Hold random celebrations! Dance! Dress up as a character! Build experiences which make people beg to come back.

Use People's Names

I (Todd) spent more than a week with Brad Gustafson, a principal in Minnesota, one summer at EdCamp Leader in Chicago. During that time, he did something that really impressed me: He used people's names. He spoke to the people working at every establishment we visited and used their names. His first question was always, "What's your name again?" Whether we were checking into a hotel, getting in a cab, or eating at a restaurant—it didn't matter. Brad always asked people their names and continued to use their names throughout the entire conversation.

So simple! And I'm convinced we consistently received better service because of it. As I watched their interactions, I realized these people had a more pleasant air about them. Why? Because they felt noticed.

Service jobs can be thankless—every other minute, someone is complaining. Brad taught me that the simple act of using a name shows you care and makes the difference between a worker feeling simply like a fixture in the establishment and feeling like an important individual.

Our kids and coworkers need to feel important, too! We know using their names makes a positive difference—because they've told us. Many kids have told us how great it is that we actually *know* their names, and this year, one of our teachers cried because, for the first time in five years, her principal had pronounced her name correctly.

Learn the names of your students and coworkers—and *use* them. It shows you care.

Learn the names of your students and coworkers—and *use* them. It shows you care.

Notice the Loners

People who attend my (Todd's) presentations or spend time with me in small group settings see me as boisterous and outgoing. In reality, I can be very introverted in large groups or crowds of people I don't know. In a room of people, I'm the person who sits in the corner sipping my water. I'll talk if you talk to me, but I won't actively seek out conversation. As a result, I can begin to feel like an outsider surrounded by people who are eagerly interacting.

Ben Gilpin, Brandon Blom, Theresa Stager, Tony Sinanis, and Melinda Miller (principals from across the country) taught me the art of continually seeking out other "loners" like me and finding ways to make them feel included. When I'd try to slink away or hide at a quiet table at an education conference, one of them would find me and either sit with me or pull me back into the circle.

In doing so, they taught me the value of doing the same for others who, in certain social settings, can feel intimidated, unworthy, or like an outsider. People need to be reminded that they belong. They need someone to reach out and pull them back in or just sit with them. Everyone wants to be noticed and feel important.

That goes for our students, too. Time after time we see kids sitting alone at lunch, playing by themselves at recess, or walking down the hall with their head held low so they don't have to look anyone in the eyes. Their body language makes it clear that they wish they could just disappear. As educators, it's our job to notice the kids who could easily go unnoticed—those whose coping mechanism is to fade into the background. We love eating with kids at lunch for this reason. We can easily walk into a lunchroom, spot the kid by himself, and sit with him. And then what happens? All the other kids want to move over and sit with us, too! And maybe—just maybe—this interaction begins to remove a few bricks from the wall between these kids.

Give People a Voice

For one conference I (Todd) attended, I set up a panel discussion but hadn't selected any of the panelists when I submitted my proposal. I'd just called it "Tech Ninja and Friends."

When I arrived at the conference, I asked a few people I knew to be part of the panel. I didn't ask the well-known presenters; I asked teachers who only missed school to attend major conferences and EdCamps. I had been greatly encouraged when someone I respected had asked me to speak with them, and I wanted to pass on the encouragement to others.

After the presentation, which was made to about 1,500 people, the wife of one of the panelists, with tears in her eyes, said to me, "Thank you for including him. It was such a big deal to him for you to ask him."

We're all in education for a reason, and we all have something incredibly worthy to share. When you have the stage, the blog, or the social media followers, make the choice to use that platform to allow others to speak and share their ideas.

Even if you don't have a huge following, you can encourage others to talk about their ideas. Start a campus blog and allow different staff members to share their stories each week. Or make a weekly video highlighting the awesome things your students are up to. Social media gives you a platform. Use it to spread good, to share awesomeness, and to encourage others to find their voices.

Favorites, Retweets, and Interactions

Through social media, I (Todd) have met people I respect immensely—people around whom, when I finally get to meet them in person, I feel shy, even though I really want to take a picture and shake their hands. Last summer, I had the honor of online (and a few face-to-face) interactions with some of these EduHeroes: Erik Wahl, Todd Whitaker, Steve Spangler, Dave Burgess, Kim Bearden, Ron Clark, Angela Maiers, Salome Thomas-EL, and others. By *favoriting* my Tweet, sharing my idea and giving me credit, and sending a "you're-doing-awesome-things" message, they had me taking screenshots of things and dancing around the house! My wife can attest to it! Just these simple actions really made a difference to me.

During one of my last keynotes of the summer, the organizer told me, "We have a lot of guest speakers, but you do something I haven't seen the others do. You give every person who talks to you the same excitement—the same attention—as the other one hundred you have talked to before them. You make each of them feel they're the most important person—like they're the first person who's come to talk to you." While I'd never thought about it much before, I know I do it for a reason. I do it because everyone deserves to feel special. I want them to leave feeling important.

We try to do the same thing at our campuses. We try to greet every kid with a warm welcome—as if they're the most important person in the world. We speak to everyone who passes us in the hall. We share smiles and give high fives. Those positive interactions are just as important for the adults on campus, too. Coworkers and parents of students should feel more important after coming into contact with us.

No matter what kind of day we're having, we feel it's important to do these things. It's our job. It's your job. Yes, at the end of a long day, it's hard to smile and interact when all you want to do is go home and relax, but that's when it's most important to do so. We love being asked, "How are you still so full of energy and happy at the end of the day?" We have to be! Every child deserves to feel important. Every child deserves to feel like the "favorite."

Every child deserves to feel important. Every child deserves to feel like the "favorite."

Visit Kids at Home

Home visits are my all-time favorite activity. When I (Adam) started visiting kids at home, it was usually because of disruptive behavior in the classroom or academic struggles we wanted to address and support. These visits have morphed over the years into celebration visits.

Sometimes I visit a student who's made huge improvement at school, either academically, socially, or with her behavior. Sometimes I visit because a child has been sad at school because parents are getting divorced, are in jail, or are traveling for work and the kids are tired of the nanny.

Whatever the reason, visiting a student at her home has an amazing impact. Sometimes I will help them clean their rooms. Read a few chapters in a book. Shoot some hoops or play catch with a football. Todd and I have seen kids with negative behaviors do a complete 180 after visiting them at home. Why? We believe it's because we've invested time with them, and they see we care about them. But we've also seen kids, who initially had more in their tanks, go from good to *great*. Our visits made them want to achieve even more.

Take the time to schedule a home visit. Kids will remember it for the rest of their lives!

Wipe down Some Tables and Take out the Trash

When I (Adam) was an assistant principal, our lunch period was *busy*! We had 1,200 kindergarten through fifth graders, and lunch lasted over two hours every day. That's a lot of kids to feed and clean up after. Yes, I wore slacks and a tie to work every day, and I still helped serve food, wipe down tables, and take out the trash.

The kids used to always ask me why I carried a rag around and picked up trash off the floor. They thought it was funny for me to serve food. But I'd always tell them, "I'm part of the team."

"But you're the assistant principal," they argued.

"I know, and I help out the team," I'd say.

When I left that school to become a principal, the head custodian gave me a huge hug as I was saying good-bye. She'd been a custodian for more than fifteen years and said I was the only administrator who'd ever wiped down a table or carried the trash to the dumpster. That really hit home with me. I didn't think it was big deal—I was just part of the team.

Everyone on your campus is important. Everyone should be listened to and feel supported and encouraged. Lend a hand and be part of the team! You should never be too high and mighty to stop and serve.

Ride the Bus

For the past few years, I've (Adam) had special day classes on my campus. Many of those students utilize the transportation system from our district and ride the bus to and from school. It really bothered me that I never got a chance to interact with those families at pick-up or drop-off.

After a few phone calls and conversations with our transportation director, I was cleared and had a date to meet the bus at 6:00 a.m. I had that jittery excitement along with uncertainty at something I'd never before done. The driver was meticulous in getting the bus ready at the depot, doing all the safety checks, and making sure we were ready for the kids.

Our drivers care 100 percent about these kids! You can hear it in their voices, see it in their actions, and notice it with everything they do. We're so lucky to have them as part of our team.

The highlight of my ride was, of course, seeing all our students in the morning at their homes. They were all *super* surprised to see me, and their parents were equally shocked. Being able to start the day with them and build a closer connection to their families was exciting in many ways.

All educators should take the time to ride the bus with their students!

Little things really can make a world of difference. We know we're not finished learning, and by no means are we experts at any of these, but we're continually practicing, continually learning, and continually getting better. Because in the end, the kids deserve it!

Things to Consider and Tweet

1. What are some "little things" you've learned?
2. Why is it important to kids for you to be continually growing?
3. What's the "biggest thing" holding you back from doing the "little things"?

#KidsDeserveIt

8 Leave It in Your Car

Your car is more important to your students than you might think. In fact, it's more important to *you* than you might realize. Why? Because your problems can either stay in your car or get out of it and come along with you. Think about these situations, which we've likely all faced at some point:

- You had a difficult morning at home.
- The commute to work was frustrating.
- You got an unsettling email from a parent last night.
- You have an upcoming meeting you're not looking forward to.
- You're not feeling well, but you're not sick enough to stay at home.
- Financial problems have you stressed.
- You had an argument with your children, spouse, or loved one.
- You're still reeling from the day before.
- You're low on gas, had a flat tire, and/or spilled coffee on your shirt.

Kids deserve an excited adult. They need someone who's ready to explore and laugh with them all day—someone who's looking for those magic moments, full of high fives coming down the line with energy radiating all around. Our kids have far more issues to deal with at home than many of us realize. School is their safety net, their safe place, their one true home. They want and *need* us to come to school every day, ready to surround them with love, encouragement, and hope.

Leave your problems in your car. Take a deep breath and focus on the positive. Find hope. Kids need the best you. Step out and be your best every single day. Be awesome! The kids deserve it!

Things to Consider and Tweet

1. If you're having a rough morning, check Twitter and search for #KidsDeserveIt for some motivation.
2. Find a colleague on the way into the building and talk about some wins they've experienced with kids lately!
3. Knowing every child in your class or school is someone else's "everything," how would you want your own "everything" to be treated?

#KidsDeserveIt

9 Dealing with Doubt

Doubt can sometimes lurk around us, but when it gets inside us, it's hard to shake loose. It raises lots of questions:

- Are we doing enough for our students and teachers to support them in their work?
- Have we connected with parents in a meaningful way to build solid relationships?
- We have too many "issues" this week; nothing positive is happening on our campus.
- Can I do this work? Am I cut out for this? Wouldn't it be easier to find a different job?
- Clearly everyone is doing a better job than I am. They have it all together.
- Maybe this isn't meant for me?
- It's just too much!

Doubts can be discouraging. We both know this feeling well, and it's gotten us down at times. So down, in fact, that we've been in dark places, trying to find the light to guide us out. And we've found that, even in the darkest moments when it seems there's no way out, there's always a light.

You can listen to the doubts, but the fact is, these kids need you! Their parents need you! Your colleagues need your energy, ideas, and excitement for learning! Teachers need your passion and mojo for creating amazing experiences for kids, which light their fire and help them burn bright! Every one of us was given amazing gifts that others around us need to hear about and learn from. Never doubt that.

YOU MATTER

My (Todd) first week as principal at Webb Elementary, in the fall of 2015, was filled with amazingness—awesome lessons from teachers, great interactions with kids and families, and exciting moments in the hallways and at recess. But it was also incredibly challenging for me.

This was a much larger campus than I'd been on the year before at Navasota Intermediate—more kids, more staff, more parents, and more grade levels. We had just expanded to a pre-K through fifth-grade campus, and with 750 kids, I was seeing even more heartache and pain—more children whose home lives broke my heart. But on top of that, due to all the changes within the district and campus, I had to deal with more venom from parents on social media and in person than I had in all my years in education combined. And it took a toll on me.

As all that stress mounted, I allowed doubt to take hold.

I often think about the power doubt holds over us. We have days we doubt if we're a good spouse, friend, brother, sister, or parent. We doubt if we're a good teacher. We doubt if we truly know what we're doing. If we're cut out for this. We doubt our talents, our skills, and our genius.

Doubt can rip us to shreds. If we let it, doubt can destroy us. Through the negativity and destructive words I read online and heard spoken to me, I began to wonder if I truly *was* that unwanted and disliked by families in my community. I started to wonder if my presence and work even mattered.

I'd been telling my team that every single one of us at Webb Elementary matters. In fact, I took time every day to remind others of their worth. It's funny how I quickly forgot my own value.

After some prayer, I did what I always advise others to do: I found my people. I sought out my friends and coeducators who knew my heart. I cried with them, prayed with them, and shared my pain and struggle. They spoke words of truth that brought me back. They built me up and reminded me who I knew I was.

Ignite a Spark of Hope

I (Adam) must admit that doubt hovers over me at times. It can linger for a few days or for weeks at a time. I try to fight it off—I always hope I can fight it off!

That feeling of being *overwhelmed* with:

- too many initiatives
- too many emails
- too many forms to submit
- too many new programs that need attention
- too many older programs not being supported adequately
- too many meetings—always too many meetings
- too much conversation about non-educational things like parking, buildings, fences, sign-in sheets, and forms
- not enough supervision
- not enough fun

- not enough time for exciting programs
- not enough time to really engage with kids.

Being at work too early, staying too late, and still not getting every-thing done is tiresome. Not seeing my family enough—knowing my balance is way off and being concerned about it—makes me wonder what's coming up next and whether I have the ability to support it.

Head above water—head below water—*repeat—repeat—repeat—repeat!*

Being overwhelmed can lead to so much doubt. But even as I strug-gle with doubt from time to time, I've learned not to allow it to take root in my life. The way to beat it is to surround yourself with others who will remind you that you matter, that your work matters, and that you are making a difference. Connect with others who will lift you up—who will help you celebrate every single success. Because even the smallest successes are worth celebrating. And those small successes can create the tiniest sparks of hope. Nurture that hope and it can grow into flames that squelch doubt and ignite your campus with a sense of possibility.

When you struggle with feelings of doubt, ask yourself: What *is* the meaningful work we're doing? What's most important? Where do we get the biggest bang for our buck?

Even the smallest successes are worth celebrating.

You'll find the answers to those questions in the classrooms—with kids, learning about what their #eduadventure is. It's talking curricu-lum with teachers and how to make kids *more* stoked about school.

It's in building relationships with parents to strengthen the home-to-school connection. But most importantly, it's in helping kids feel confident—showing them what's possible to achieve—showing them we believe in and care about them!

So when you feel doubt creep in, tell it to back off! Look at yourself in the mirror and remind yourself how incredibly unique and important you are. And then connect to others who can support you! Please connect with us on Twitter or Voxer. We need you! You need us! None of us can do this job alone—we need to support each other!

Things to Consider and Tweet

1. What makes you doubt or question your abilities?
2. How do you fight the feeling of doubt?
3. Who are the people that support you? Take some time to recognize them, celebrate them, and thank them.

#KidsDeserveIt

10 Everyone Needs a Cheerleader

If you've worked with kids for any amount of time, you know the battles they face. The more we've worked with kids, the more we've seen how many of them don't have someone cheering them on. Telling them how amazing they are. Believing in them. Giving them gentle nudges forward.

When you dive into the biographies of successful people—any celebrity, athlete, author, artist, politician, or business owner—you will find that many of them give credit for their success to someone who invested time and effort in them when they were growing up. Someone who cheered for them.

We have to figure out ways to build up and champion our students—to let them know we love them—no matter what. We believe in them and will stand by them. We will be their cheerleaders! One of our favorite TED Talks is Rita Pierson's "Every Kid Needs a Champion." She tells about grading a student's paper and writing "+2" on the paper because he got two answers right. She said, "You see, 'minus eighteen' sucks all the life out of you. 'Plus two' says, 'I ain't all bad.'"[1] Build others up!

Growing up was full of ups and downs for me (Todd). I grew up in a house full of turmoil. My parents fought every day, my dad drank daily, and he wasn't home very much. I never felt like I fit in anywhere. While I don't remember a lot about my childhood, one thing I do remember quite well is my grandmother.

Throughout my childhood, no matter what was going on, my grandmother was always my rock. My brother and I visited my grandmother and grandfather almost every weekend. Grandma cooked meal after meal with me, and she taught me everything I know about cooking. She instilled in me a love of reading, and every time I visited, she took me to the bookstore to get the next book in the *Animorphs* series. She taught me how to use Microsoft Word and Excel, and had me make my own business cards. She was the person I wanted most to like my wife before we were married. Most of all, my grandmother was my cheerleader.

Every single time I visited her house, my grandmother told me how special I was. She told me how much I meant to her. She told me that no matter what anyone said, I was going to do great things. And in my childish innocence, I believed her. I felt like I was the most important person in the world every moment I spent with her.

During high school and college, I continued to build my relationship with my grandmother. I called her every time something great happened in my life, and she would celebrate me! She made me cut out every article I was mentioned in and save every project or paper I did at school. Then she would take the article or item *everywhere* she went and tell people how proud of me she was. Every time I was with my grandmother outside of her house, she would make sure to tell someone, "Do you know who this is? This is my grandson, Todd.

---

1 Rita Pierson, "Rita Pierson: Every Kid Needs a Champion," TED video, 7:48, filmed May 2013, https://www.ted.com/talks/rita_pierson_every_kid_needs_a_champion?language=en.

And he's going to change the world!" Part of me was embarrassed, but another part of me was exploding with pride because someone was so proud of me.

When I started my career, my grandmother was the first person I called to share the good news about each achievement. She always told me she was so proud of me and so excited for me—even if she had no understanding of what I had accomplished. When I visited, she would always ask me, "What amazing things are you doing now to change the world?"

In the middle of my sixth year of teaching, my grandmother was diagnosed with pancreatic cancer. My grandmother is a fighter—she didn't put up with anything from anyone. So when she was diagnosed, she vowed to fight with everything in her. And she did.

But after fighting for almost a year and half, she wore out. She got tired of fighting. My grandfather called to tell me he'd taken her to the hospital because she'd refused to eat or take her medicine. He didn't know how long she would live, and she wasn't talking to anyone.

I drove up right away. I sat by her bed, held her hand, and told her how much I loved her. She was lying with her eyes closed, breathing slowly. I moved to give her a hug and tell her goodbye, when I saw her eyes open. She whispered to me, "Goodbye, Todd. I'm so proud of you. I'm sorry." It took everything in me not to break down and fall apart on the spot. I was determined to stay strong, but telling her goodbye was the hardest thing I'd ever had to do.

That was the last time I saw my grandmother alive. She passed away about a week later, and my grandfather asked if I would do the eulogy at her funeral. How could I say no? I wanted to honor my grandmother. I can remember that day like it was yesterday. Standing in the front of a church full of people, talking about what an incredible woman my grandmother was, I broke down in tears—something I never do in front of people.

The most important thing my grandmother taught me is the

importance of having someone to cheer us on. My grandmother was always the one person I knew would celebrate me and build me up. There are still times I catch myself grabbing my phone to call her and share my good news. I miss her often, but I want to continually carry on what she taught me. I want to celebrate those around me who are doing great things. I want to remind them of how important they are in this world, how much I believe in them, and how much I care. Because that's what my grandmother did for me.

Champion Kids

My (Adam) four-year-old daughter loves playing on monkey bars. We're always looking for new parks to try out more monkey bars. We went to my friend's school one morning where there were some super long bars. She spotted them from across the yard and rode her bike over.

"Dad, I want to try those monkeys!"

"You bet, let's go."

She climbed the ladder...

"Dad, I'm nervous, I can't. Hold my legs the entire way."

"No way, Greta. You can do it! Let's go!"

"I can't..."

"Yes, you can! Now make it happen!"

And she did! All on her own—with my encouragement! How did she feel? Empowered, confident, special, *proud*—she felt as if she could attempt anything.

All she needed was a cheerleader.

I'm starting to think lack of success is not so much about the fear of failure, but more a lack of encouragement. We need each other. Nobody can do it alone.

We must believe in our kids!

We must encourage our kids!

We must push our colleagues!

We have to encourage those around us!

We're so much better together if we all believe in ourselves and push each other as well!

We have the power to tear down or build up the children who walk into our lives every day. Sadly, so many of the kids we serve don't believe we really care.

Students will push you emotionally, fight against you, and test you. Why? Because they've been let down so many times in their lives that they think if they push you hard enough, you'll walk away and give up on them, too.

Please don't give up on them! Champion kids. Celebrate them. Love them unconditionally. Be their cheerleaders. All kids deserve it!

We have the power to tear down or build up the children who walk into our lives every day.

Things to Consider and Tweet

1. Who was your cheerleader when you were growing up?
2. Whom have you positively impacted with your words and actions?
3. How can we ensure we're making an impact that matters?

#KidsDeserveIt

11 What's Your Message?

What we say, how we act, and the way we carry ourselves send a message. The message may be so subtle that we don't realize it. Or it may be so common, it has become a habit. For example, if you see a certain student or coworker in the hallway and think something negative, your body language sends a message. Or when you're eating lunch in the staff room with the people who have a habit of complaining, and you hop on the negativity train. You may think that chiming in doesn't matter. You may even rationalize: *What are a few comments going to hurt? Everyone complains in here, anyway*. But your contribution to that conversation sends a message.

We have to admit that we also occasionally fall into "complaining mode." But one thing we've worked really hard to do is surround ourselves with people who will speak the truth to us and let us know when we need an attitude adjustment.

Now don't get us wrong. We all have those really difficult days where we need to just "vent." Days when we need to get things off of our chest. That's fine! Just make sure that when you do vent, it's to people who are close to you and who can provide a listening ear and some perspective.

We know that people become like those they spend the most time with, so be intentional about who's in your space. The right people won't be afraid to call you out when you start looking at problems without offering solutions. Surround yourself with people who will call you out when you're wallowing in negativity and will help you find the silver lining.

School and classroom leaders control the mood of their environment. Others quickly pick up on negativity and complaining. It kills the mood, it drags others down, and most of all, it pushes others away. We have to set the example.

Someone is watching every move you make and listening to every word you speak. That's why it's so important to be aware of the message you're sending out with your body language, choices, and words.

It's so easy to complain, to whine, or to point out everything that's wrong. But what if we sent a different message? What if we focused on what we *could* control? What if we spent more time building others up instead of tearing them down? What if we looked for solutions instead of complaining about what's wrong? What if we took time to see past the situation and spent time trying to understand what's underneath?

When you take the time to really listen and understand someone's beliefs, experiences, and story, then you're telling them that what they've been through is important and that it matters. Our lives and our world move so quickly that we often forget to just stop and take the time to sit and listen. Give people—your colleagues and students—the opportunity to let you into their world.

What message are you sending? Kids can hear, see, and feel your message—even if you think they can't. They even pick up a message when you don't say anything at all. Standing idly by in silence sends a powerful message.

Make your message profound. Make your message positive. Make your message student–centered. Make your message about growth, learning—and awesomeness!

Send a positive message. Your kids deserve it!

What if we looked for solutions instead of complaining about what's wrong?

Things to Consider and Tweet

1. How can you turn the negative comments you hear into positive messages?
2. How can you celebrate or recognize those who send a positive message?
3. How do you protect yourself from getting sucked into someone else's negative message?

#KidsDeserveIt

12 The Truth about Bullies

We hear about bullying all the time in education, but bullying didn't just start recently. We probably all remember getting picked on in some way as a child. Either because of our size, our friends, our extracurricular activities, our personality, or our voice. You name it—we've all been there.

Do you remember what it felt like as a child to be called names? We do. We remember what it's like to get to a point when the bully's words start to sound like the truth. It can take a long time to be able to look back and realize that the awful things said about you were never true. It may be even harder to realize the things said were coming from a place of hurt from within the bully.

When Bullies Grow Up

I (Todd) never experienced bullying as an adult until I became an administrator. Sure, as a teacher, people had said mean, hurtful, untrue things about me. Everyone sometimes deals with that. And I knew that, as a school leader, not everyone would be happy with everything I did. I knew I would make some people upset no matter what choice I made. I'd done that as a teacher, and I sort of expected to disappoint more people as an administrator.

Funny thing, though … the bullying didn't come from a parent or a student! The bullying came from someone closer—someone who used to be involved in what was happening at our school.

To have someone text me, over and over and over again, the most hateful, untrue, and damaging things I've heard in years—to call me ungodly, clearly not a Christian, a liar, stupid, clueless, damaging, and so much worse—was something I never dreamed I would have to deal with. To have multiple members of my family and staff brought into the mix by this person—I just couldn't comprehend it.

Through all of it, I chose to remain silent. I didn't respond to any texts or any messages. I didn't want to get involved in a war of words. But I was reminded again how pain can come out when someone is in an unhappy place. And I have always believed that "hurting people hurt people." And in the end, the bullying stopped. It didn't happen overnight. In fact, it took almost a year. But I learned that not getting involved in a war of words, and instead blocking that person through electronic communication avenues, was the best decision I could have made in that situation. It also impacted us as a campus. My team quickly learned that I wasn't going to allow someone from the outside (or inside) to destroy us, and that I wasn't going to even entertain the drama. Our kids needed us to focus on *them*. And that's just what we did! I also had the peace of mind of knowing I didn't play into any of the bullying, and instead, chose to take the high road and learn from the experience.

Even Teachers Bully

When I (Adam) was a classroom teacher, I always spent time at recess and lunch hanging out with my students. Inevitably, other kids would also come around to join us in a game of football, four-square, or just chat when I was in the yard. One student always talked to me, gave high fives, and really connected with me. I could tell he was a kid who needed some attention. We clicked right away, and he wasn't even in my class.

He was in another third-grade class and was struggling. His teacher was always barking at him and sending him outside the classroom. In my opinion, the teacher was being a bully. I wanted to advocate for the student because I believed the teacher's treatment was unfair; no child should ever be treated disrespectfully by an educator.

In May, our principal told us we'd have a third- and fourth-grade combination class the following year and asked for volunteers to teach it. No hands went up. After the meeting, I told him I'd teach the class. He was ecstatic. I only had one condition: I wanted this student in my class. If he wasn't put in my class, I wouldn't teach the combo.

All conferences should include some celebration of the kids and their strengths.

Fast-forward to the following year and our first parent-teacher conference, which included this student, because I always had my students attend their conferences. I was telling his mom and dad how amazing he was, how much I loved his ideas, his energy, his passion, etc. His mom started crying right in front of us.

When it was time for the student to step outside so his parents and I could talk in private, he was glowing. Clearly, prior conferences hadn't gone like this. Personally, I think all conferences should include some celebration of the kids and their strengths. The point, after all, is to maximize their strengths—not bring them down.

When their boy had left the room, I told his parents I'd intentionally recruited their child for my class—that it had been non-negotiable because I wanted to take him under my wing. They couldn't believe it, but I told them that's why I became an educator—to help kids thrive.

Quite a few years later, this student came to visit me. He was a senior in high school, applying to college, and waiting to hear back from those schools. This time, I was the one in tears. Seeing kids grow and become their best is still the reason I'm an educator. *We must encourage our kids, support them, and help them achieve all their potential!*

We write this chapter not to share our pain, but in the hope that as you read this, you'll think about the things you say to others. The things you text to others. The things you write about others. We all get hurt by others, but we don't have to lash out and continue the pain. No matter how strong a resolve the belittled person has, she will eventually begin to doubt her worth. We've been there. We've doubted our worth and started doubting what we were doing. We come from years of being picked on and called out. We know what it feels like. We know the lasting marks it leaves.

We've learned you can allow the messages you receive to define you, *or* you can surround yourself with people who know you and truly care about you. The road through bullying isn't easy. The scars don't ever completely heal, but you can learn from them. One of the biggest lessons we've learned is to continually show love because, in the end, love will always conquer hate. The other big takeaway from our bullying ordeals has been forgiveness. We've learned to give it freely and often. We've been forgiven far more than we have ever deserved. So how could we not forgive those who hurt us? We have to. Forgiveness isn't about freeing the offender; it's about freeing ourselves.

We must encourage our kids, support them, and help them achieve all their potential!

Things to Consider and Tweet

1. What hurt or belief are you still holding on to because of what someone said to you or about you?
2. Have you experienced the freedom of forgiveness? What did it do for you?
3. In what ways have you shown love or resilience in the midst of anger or hurt?
4. How can we use personal lessons about bullying to teach our kids?

#KidsDeserveIt

13 Put the Bat in Their Hands

They can't write in kindergarten.

They're too young to code.

Why would you teach fifth graders how to Tweet?

First graders blogging? They can hardly spell correctly!

We can't unblock those sites—the kids will do bad things.

Maybe your students can do those things, but mine can't.

I'm uncomfortable with those tools. My students don't need to use them.

He can't even read a book! Why would he be interested in building a circuit board?

I can't take my students outside to learn. They need to be in the right environment.

If I give them an iPad, they might break it.

If I don't lecture all the time, they won't learn correct strategies to pass that test.

Excuses. Unbelief. Limitations.

Far too often, our students aren't the ones who limit themselves. We do. We tell them what we think they can and can't handle. We tell them what we believe they're capable of.

It Started with Coding

I (Adam) started teaching a coding class four years ago when coding wasn't even really that big. It started with an idea, the hope of getting kids involved with writing code, and seeing what they could do. Could they handle it?

I threw a Google Form together and shared it with our school community. I wasn't quite sure if any kids would sign up to meet in our computer lab one day a week at 7:00 a.m. To my absolute delight, twenty-eight students signed up for our class. I really didn't know what I was doing, to be completely honest. I did know that the kids were super excited to be learning alongside me, and all I really did was give them access and encouragement.

Fast-forward a few years, and it's hard to imagine what my school would be like without coding. Coding is just the beginning; it's the start of a forward-thinking, innovative mindset. Coding isn't about computers, it's about giving kids access to relevant ideas and projects. It's about opening doors for kids to see what they're capable of.

Start a coding club or team on your campus and ignite the love of learning and exploration!

Believe and Empower

Imagine what kids could do if we stopped limiting them and put the bat in their hands instead. With our coaching and support, they'd knock anything they tried out of the park! But you will never see what kids can actually do unless you let them try.

We must believe in kids—and empower them. We must be in the business of removing boundaries for kids and opening all available doors for them. We have to give them a voice. We have to move kids out of the *dugout* and onto the *field*. We need to see what they *can* do instead of assuming what they *can't*.

We must be in the business of removing boundaries for kids.

How much potential is never reached because adults say "no," or "can't," or "shouldn't," or "won't," or "You're not old enough"? How much potential is missed simply because adults don't take time to listen to kids? First Timothy 4:12 of the Bible says, "And don't let anyone put you down because you're young. Teach with your life: by word, by demeanor, by love, by faith, by integrity."[1]

Educators need to refuse to say "no," "can't," "shouldn't," "won't," or "You're not old enough," and we should *always* be listening to kids. We should want the absolute best for our students. Sometimes this means relinquishing some control, taking the bat out of our own hands, and putting it in theirs. Give them a chance to hit a home run. They deserve it.

---

1   1 Timothy 4:12 (The Message).

Things to Consider and Tweet

1. How can you open doors for kids to help them reach their full potential?
2. Believing they'll find a way to do them, what higher-grade-level activities could you modify for younger students?
3. What can you do if your leadership doesn't support letting kids take some control?

#KidsDeserveIt

14 You Never Know

Everyone has a story. Some stories are longer than others and filled with heartache and pain. Some are full of privilege and love. But we all have stories to share. We're all filled with feelings, personalities, hopes, dreams, and often, battles we're fighting which others know nothing about.

This is definitely true of our students. How many of the students who walk by you each morning came from a house filled with chaos just ten minutes before they arrived at school? Or dealt with chaos the night before? Or have dealt with chaos for the past two weeks? How many came to school from situations where parents are yelling, or the parents are divorced? They didn't sleep well. They're stressed from pressure they feel at home or at school. Maybe their parents are traveling for work, and they miss their family. Some are fighting with siblings.

Others don't feel connected at school. They're having trouble with friends at school. They don't have any friends *at all*. School is too hard for them. School is too easy for them. Kids are mean to them. Their teacher isn't very nice.

They didn't eat breakfast. They didn't eat breakfast *or* dinner last night. A sibling has special needs, and it's hard for them to cope. They don't look like everyone else at school and feel left out at times. They don't feel like anyone cares about them. They couldn't finish their homework because they had to cook for their family the night before. Their job is to wake up first and get all their siblings ready every morning. The electricity was turned off again. The water stopped. There was another shooting on the street. There are no clean clothes in the house. Dad left again. Mom left again. Their favorite pet died. Their parents told them they were stupid…

And what if no one even notices them when they walk down the hall?

As educators, it's our responsibility to be nice and acknowledge others. More than that, it's our honor to talk with kids and listen to them, to sit on the floor with them when needed, to eat lunch with them.

How many of the students who walk by you each morning came from a house filled with chaos just ten minutes before they arrived at school?

Connecting with kids and their parents, being visible, creating opportunities for student voice, and amplifying that voice—this is our joy. It's our privilege to care about kids—a *lot*—to show kids how much they matter to this world, to boost their confidence and make them all feel famous. Our job is to focus on kids, not spreadsheets, and to be awesome all of the time. And we can do all of this if we remember why we went into education in the first place!

We must have intentional, positive interactions with our students because we just don't know what they're experiencing—and we just don't know how or when our interactions with them might make a positive difference in their lives.

But we can do this with more than just our students. Imagine the positive changes in your school if every adult was a little more intentional about noticing and valuing others. Imagine how everyone would feel, knowing they're an important part of something.

We've both experienced the immense power in saying "hello" to everyone we walk by at school. Sharing a smile. Taking the time to ask how a student's day was going. Even more importantly, we've experienced the power in taking the time to listen to the student's answer.

You never know the power of a simple word or action. The smallest stone dropped into the largest lake will leave ripples felt miles away. We can't undervalue our impact, our reach, and our potential. We have to remember to listen, be positive, and treat everyone how we want to be treated! Go the extra mile. Kids will benefit, teachers will benefit, and families will benefit!

Adam has a poster in his office which is a daily reminder for us, for teachers, for parents, and for students: "Work Hard and Be Nice to People." But we think there's even more to it. The poster should also contain the words: "Because, You Never Know!"

Things to Consider and Tweet

1. How have you firsthand felt the power of being noticed? How did you feel? How did it change you?
2. Share a time when you invested in someone and then felt the "ripples."
3. Take time today to build up someone you work with. Share the creative way you did it!

#KidsDeserveIt

15 I Wish You Knew...

ust like everyone has a story we may never know about, there are also stories people wish we knew. Everyone has a story. Everyone has a side they wish more people understood. We believe in the power of giving others a voice. So we gave voice to administrators, teachers, parents, and students from around the world. We sent out a Google Form via email, blog posts, Twitter, Facebook, and other social media outlets to gather as many varied responses as we could. We asked the simple question: What do you wish more people knew about your role?

The answers were powerful—some were even heartbreaking.

From Kids

I wish you knew:

- I will do anything to fit in with my peers, but I still really want you (my teacher) to like me.
- some of us cling to our cell phones during class because the people we're connecting with provide us a safe space this class has never provided.
- we're bullied by smirks, snickers, and raised eyebrows more than by verbal taunts or physical means. You can't do much to stop it, but you can help students like me who walk around with our eyes down and our headphones blasting so the music drowns out everyone around us.
- my story. I'd be happy to tell you if you'd just ask.
- how much I like having you as a teacher.
- how hard I work for barely passing grades.
- how to pronounce my name.
- we'd like you to interact with us like we're family.
- it can be hard to make school a priority when I'm thinking about problems in my family. Please be someone who understands.
- how much I miss my sister. Sometimes I'm really sad—sometimes for the whole day.
- this classroom is the only place I feel safe.
- a lot of us are going through tough times.
- we need your constant support.
- we need you to understand we do have busy schedules just like you.
- everyone's special no matter what religion, color, or race they are.

From Parents

I wish you knew:

- how much it means to me when you *want* to know about my child—what makes him tick, what gets him excited, or what makes him sad.

- a little bit about my child's background—like how his two brothers never came home from the hospital, or how his daddy has to travel for work—and how to apply that understanding to counseling him.

- my child is my everything, and I do expect you to leave the proverbial flock to find him if he has gone astray.

- I support you, especially when you're supporting my child.

- really take time to know my child. Knowing him has changed my life.

- I dread homework. I want to spend quality time with my child after a long day at work. I would rather read with her, help her where she is behind, teach her to cook, or work on our own learning projects. Instead, we fight with each other over hours of pointless busywork each night. I wish you knew that homework this year is damaging the relationship I have with my child. I wish we could look forward to homework each night.

- she is not just an "ADHD kid." She is intelligent, creative, and wonderful. Her brain just moves faster than her body can keep up. She is so much more than a label.

- there are times when life gets in the way of me being my child's first teacher. I know it is my responsibility to teach my child in every aspect, but sometimes I don't take advantage of a teachable moment because it doesn't occur to me at that exact moment that I should teach her.

- I *am* teaching my child manners, but sometimes she just doesn't obey. I'm not a bad parent, and she's not a bad child. She makes mistakes and her attention span *is* shorter than ours.

- I really do appreciate and value all the hard work teachers do to instill knowledge into my kid's life and the ways they encourage him to be a better person. It really means a lot when teachers keep us updated on what they are doing with my kids on a daily basis.

- how much I can see some teachers and staff trying harder than others.

- the feeling I have every day when my child comes home, discouraged because the other girls are continually chipping away her confidence. We have tried everything to make her understand it's not her, but the pain is real to her.

From Teachers

I wish you knew:

- I try my best each day, each week, each month, and each year to help every student grow academically, socially, and emotionally. Sometimes I feel like my best isn't enough.

- I wake up in the middle of the night thinking about ways to help your child.

- I *wanted* to be a teacher. I didn't become one because, as some people joke, "I couldn't think of anything better to do," or "I wasn't smart enough to do something better."

- how much time I spend away from my own family to make sure the 120 kids I teach have an opportunity to shine, grow, and succeed.

- I want my students to be brave and bold and try new things. I want them never to be afraid to make mistakes, because their brave actions might inspire others to try new things. Their actions may show others it is okay to make mistakes; it is how we learn.

- we become a family with our students. We're all in this really hard thing together. Sometimes, we laugh; sometimes, want to give up. But we're a team.

- the most important thing: how much I truly love the kids I teach.

  - I love when the light of knowledge is switched on in a student.

  - I love the student who doesn't care because I know I can make a difference.

  - I love the student who is bored because I know I can get his attention.

  - I love the student who is passionate because I know I can ignite his zeal to learn.

  - I love the student with a dozen accommodations because I know I can find a way to break through.

  - I love the student who is a discipline problem because I know all she wants is to be heard and understood.

  - I love your kids as my own and want nothing more than to build life-long learners who love others.

  - I love *all* my students. I have never forgotten what it's like to be a kid. The most important thing I wanted as a kid was to be loved. So I love, respect, and treat my students the same way I wish I'd been loved when I was young.

  - Love is the most powerful and positive emotion, and I am extremely fortunate to give love freely through teaching.

- I lie awake at 2:00 a.m., agonizing over things I can't fix: your child's progress, my lack of patience, an email from an angry parent, a better way to teach the lesson I taught yesterday. The worrying does nothing but undermine my confidence and give me heartburn. But I want you to know that I *care*.

- when I look into your child's eyes, I see my own children. I know you're hoping your child will be nurtured and valued when you send her off to school. I strive to do that every day.

- just because we don't have a classroom full of kids in the summer doesn't mean we're not working all summer! We are always thinking about and buying stuff for our classroom. We never stop thinking about and praying for our students—even five years after we've taught them.

We're all in this really hard thing together. Sometimes, we laugh; sometimes, want to give up. But we're a team.

FROM ADMINISTRATION

I wish you knew:

- I can make a bigger difference if Central Office Administration would allow me the flexibility to try new, risky ideas with my campus. I want to do things differently, but I cannot if they don't allow me the opportunity to take risks and bring more innovation into the classrooms. Also, I can't make changes if my administration isn't willing to make changes itself.

- we never stop thinking about your kids—both their successes and their struggles. Sometimes we have to make a difficult telephone call home, but we never give up hope, even if you think we might.

- our work is hard. Our tasks are always secondary to the tasks of those we serve. Breaks are rare, and lunchtime frequently comes after students have been dismissed. Our days never play out the way we plan them. Days, weeks, months, and years all pass very quickly.

- we aren't perfect. We do the best we can with the information and resources we have. We want to be better—do more. We care about kids and hope our actions and decisions reflect that.

- our job is a lot of fun—one of the best jobs in the world. Even in the hard times, I can't imagine any other job I would enjoy more than being a building principal.

- how hard it is to be in classrooms, but not be able to *teach* in them. Even though we get plenty of opportunities to interact with kids, there is something special about having your own classroom of students to develop a unique relationship with. Teachers should cherish this opportunity and know we're jealous!

- how much more I wish I could do to reward our teachers. Their work is so valuable.

- how lonely the administrator job can feel at times.

- I am trying as hard as I can to prioritize tasks well. I'm working to improve and am progressing each month and semester.

- I'm in awe of what teachers are able to do on a daily basis.

- I have rarely had a full night's sleep in the last three years. My mind is weighed down by what I *could* do, *should've* done, *wish* I'd done, *want* to do next, what I'm *not doing* right *now*, what I wish I *could have said.* It is both exhilarating and exhausting at the same time!

- I understand your "major issue" is important to you. It's important to me. But please remember I have fifty other people's "major issues" fighting for my time and attention.

- we often feel responsible for everything that goes on in the building. This can lead to spreading ourselves thin, or sometimes not giving you the time you'd like.

- there may be times when you're the first person we see we after we've been hit, kicked, or screamed at. While we will always try to stay positive, there will be times when we slip. Please forgive us when this happens.

- we sometimes feel helpless and powerless. We want to help, but some things are out of our control. A teacher shares heartbreaking news from her personal life. Or a hard-to-reach student who is finally beginning to experience small successes tells us he is moving to a new school. Or parents raise legitimate concerns regarding safety in our parking lot—concerns which stem from other parents not following expectations or being courteous. This helplessness is the hardest part of our job—the part that keeps us awake at night.

- we wish parents would come to us personally when they're upset about a tough decision we have made, rather than using social media to complain about it.

- principals are people, too. They make mistakes, they have feelings, and while they are charged with working with and meeting the needs of a large number of stakeholders, their needs matter, too. It is a lonely seat. Principals need support, encouragement, and cheerleaders. When things are going well, everyone wants to be part of the principal's team. When things are not going so well, the principal is the first to be abandoned.

Things to Consider and Tweet

1. What is the one thing you wish people knew?

#KidsDeserveIt

16 Our Favorite Things

What do you love about being in education? We have a few things we love—"favorite things" which allow us to connect with kids:

Lunch. If you want to learn about your school, sit at the lunch tables with kids and talk with them. This is a great place *not* to be "just the adult." When we first started doing this, the kids weren't sure how to take it. But it only took a few lunch visits for them to realize we were just hanging out to chat! Sit with kids and listen. It's powerful—and fun!

Recess. Kickball, knock-out, four-square! You name it—we love recess. It's a great place to see kids on a different level. We can also take care of little discipline issues and help guide kids to make better choices. Lately, kids have been wanting to race us. They talk tons of trash about being faster than we are. They're not—we always win!

Social Media Interns. Social media interns have totally changed how we view digital citizenship and how educators should be teaching it to our kids. We're on Twitter throughout the day, and it's exciting to see a Tweet pop up on our school accounts that we didn't send.

Morning Drop-Off. We *love* morning drop-off and greeting all of our students with a smile, wave, high five, fist bump, or a hug when needed. On really special days, we wear our mascot costume—a new favorite thing! Every principal needs a mascot costume!

Learning Environment. Kids don't need to be sitting at a desk to learn and collaborate. We love it when our students sit on the floor or even take their learning outside on the grass where their discovery continues! Get creative with your learning environment. Choose a place in which you would have wanted to learn as a kid!

Get creative with your learning environment. Choose a place in which you would have wanted to learn as a kid!

Go Riding! Riding tricycles, scooters, bikes, or roller blades around campus is one of our favorite things! Kids go absolutely crazy when they see this for the first time—and so do parents!

Reading. Reading to classes is the *best*! We choose a different book each month and read to every class on campus. Kids get so excited about each new book we read. This is definitely one of our favorite things!

Recognize Awesomeness. We love to put encouraging notes in colleagues' boxes, sticky notes on their doors, or send them a quick email—anything to highlight the positive things they're doing. Taking time to recognize them for their greatness is so important! But it's also important to recognize the kiddos' awesomeness as well. Take time out of each day to find one child being awesome. Then call home to celebrate him!

Listen. Take time to listen. There is such power in just sitting and allowing someone to share his story. We love to hear what's going on in our colleagues' and students' lives. Take a few minutes to ask someone how their day is going—and mean it. Then really listen to their answer.

Positive Impact. Our "all-time favorite" thing about being in education is the opportunity we have each day to make a positive impression on kids. We love talking with kids, supporting them, laughing with them, guiding them, giving them high fives, and helping to correct them. We love being surrounded by so much amazing energy!

Things to Consider and Tweet

1. What are your favorite things about being an educator?
2. Which one of our favorite things do you think you'd like to try today? This week? This month?
3. What have you seen someone else do that you've been itching to try yourself?

#KidsDeserveIt

17 Relationships Matter Most

Relationships have always been, and will always be, of the utmost importance in our schools. They are the catalyst of our work. We've all seen kids who will move heaven and earth for a teacher they like. Students will reach new heights when they're relaxed and know you care. So we must make all kids feel special, valued, and important.

Strong relationships must be at the forefront of what you do each day on your campus. This is the only way trust can be built. And those relationships must be cultivated with all stakeholders—kids, staff, and parents—in order to fuel your school culture so it burns bright for everyone. Strong relationships can change an organization.

> ## Strong relationships must be at the forefront of what you do each day on your campus.

But it's important to remember that everyone can sense when someone is being fake. You have to be real! Some of our favorite ways to build, foster, and grow relationships are:

- First and foremost, know the names of your students—and use them!
- Talk positively about kids—all the time.
- Only make decisions which are good for them!
- Celebrate small moments.
- Talk to kids like they're a person (they'll respect you more if you do).
- Recognize genius.
- Give high fives, fist bumps, hugs, etc.
- Say "yes."
- Smile!
- Ask for others' opinions.
- Create a school motto which lets everyone know what the school's about.
- Call home, or mail home notes for celebrations on a weekly basis.
- Believe that *everyone* can achieve greatness.
- Send notes to staff members' families, recognizing the hard work each staff member does.
- Eat lunch with kids and staff.
- Play at recess.
- Talk about what you believe in and stand for. People want to follow someone with a solid plan.
- Be present.
- Have a servant's heart.

- Use Twitter, Facebook, and Instagram to showcase all the amazingness going on at your school.
- Take time to invest in face-to-face conversations.

GOING TO THEM

When I (Todd) became an administrator, I knew I had walls to tear down. I knew that the school I had been hired to lead had a "reputation." I knew the district had a "reputation." I knew that it wasn't going to be an easy road to change.

Working in my local area, I quickly learned that no matter how much I begged parents to attend an event or how much food I promised at that event, the turnout was never large. It was partly because many of my students' parents had two or three jobs, and partly because the parents didn't want to be at the school.

Through mission work in my youth, I remembered that the best way to reach someone is to go where they are. Just like you can't sit in the church and expect people to show up, you can't sit at the school and expect parents to show up.

So I had an idea. I connected with the junior high principal down the street, and we saw that our greatest areas of need were at the local apartment complexes. Those were the families we had the hardest time reaching.

So instead of begging them to come to school, our staff as well as the staff from the junior high, went to them. We used campus funds to purchase tons of hot dogs and all the fixings. We used a giant grill, and one evening we pulled up in the parking lot of the largest apartment complex and cooked free hot dogs for everyone there.

No strings. No pamphlets. No asking them to read at home or volunteer their time at school. None of it. We were just there to serve.

I remember the first time we did it and the questions we got. So many people asked, "Why are you doing this?" All we told them was, "We're from two of the schools here in town and we just wanted to tell you how much we cared about you and loved your kiddos."

We had hugs. We had tears. We had fun and laughter. Our first event served almost 300 people. We had kids running through the yards and our teachers were there to play with them, love on them, and spend time with them.

We partnered with several local businesses to help donate some of the supplies. But in the end, it was the time and effort that paid off. We gained so much ground with so many parents because they saw that we were willing to stop and take our own time, time outside of school, to serve them. And that we weren't asking for anything in return.

We continue to do cookouts to this day in each of the apartment complexes in town. It's an incredible bonding experience and a great opportunity to be a servant to others.

The biggest thing I can share is the power of servant leadership. We have to remember that we are here to serve our students' families. Sometimes it may require us giving up some of our time and resources to provide a hot meal or a few minutes of football out in the yard. But it's in those moments that real relationships are formed. It's in those moments that someone feels like they're really cared about. It's in those moments you change lives.

Things to Consider and Tweet

1. How do *you* build relationships?
2. What are your favorite ways to build relationships with kids and get to know them?
3. How do you connect with those who are really guarded and don't want to let anyone get close?
4. What is a creative way you celebrate others?

#KidsDeserveIt

18 Never Stop

Our jobs are challenging. Some days, it seems as if there are no wins—just a bunch of missed field goals and overtime losses. Being an educator is exhausting, even deflating at times. And there are days we want to leave and not come back. But every day we return, we prove to them—the children whose stories make our hearts break—that we're there for them.

Kids have asked us, "Will you come back tomorrow?" as we've walked them to their cars in the afternoon. Teachers have come to us in tears at the beginning of the year, wondering why their students ask them daily if they're coming back the next day. Heart-breaking. We can't walk away. We can't imagine abandoning these children, so quitting isn't an option. We're going to be here—standing tall, proud, and bravely for these kids who need us—these kids who have no one else willing to fight for them.

What do we teach kids if we quit? That it's okay to just quit when things get hard or when you don't agree with something? What if Thomas Edison had quit after the first hundred times his light bulb didn't work—when others told him he was crazy? What if Martin Luther King, Jr. had quit when others told him he was worthless, when he questioned the impact he was having, or when his country's system was broken? What if Oprah Winfrey had quit because no one else like her was on television, because she was overweight, or because times were hard when she didn't get the ratings?

But these people—and many more like them—*didn't* quit and changed history because of it.

Teaching is like climbing a mountain with an extremely heavy pack on … during a snow storm. The battles we have to fight, the testing, the paperwork, the absent parents, the helicopter parents, the lack of funding, the poverty—the conditions and circumstances incomprehensible to those who aren't in education. But we didn't choose to become educators because it was easy. We chose to become educators so we could change lives and impact future generations.

We chose to become educators so we could change lives and impact future generations.

So no matter how hard the challenge is, we must continue climbing. Lace up those boots and push yourself. We must keep climbing for kids.

And every once in a while, during the fray, when it's easy to focus on what isn't going well—what needs to change—stop! Look around. Take a moment to refocus your attention and regain your perspective.

And then get to climbing again. Kids deserve every ounce of energy, enthusiasm, passion, motivation, caring, and creativity we can muster. Be awesome for them, because we mean more to them than we realize. Our most important job is to love kids and convince them they are absolutely incredible and unique—to remind them they matter. Academics are a bonus!

So on those rough and difficult days when you aren't sure you can continue even one more day, lean down and look into a child's eyes. See the hope they have. See the longing of their question: "Will you come back for me tomorrow?" And answer with a resounding YES. Your kids deserve it!

Things to Consider and Tweet

1. What's a strategy you use to keep going when you want to quit?
2. How do you garner support from colleagues to push on?
3. Take time today to list all the reasons you became an educator and the experiences which have affirmed that you made the right decision. On those tough days, pull out that list as a reminder.

#KidsDeserveIt

19 Head Held High

Every educator faces the dark night when he feels like an utter failure. No matter how important it is to keep going when things go wrong, sometimes it's easier said than done.

KEEP GOING

I (Todd) took over a reconstituted campus for the 2014-2015 school year and worked alongside my tireless staff to change the course of the campus. We utilized technology, connected with others from around the world, and most importantly, we were able to teach our kids how much each one of them mattered. Children whose spirits were beaten down and who felt worthless came to believe something totally different. We taught them they were each a genius who deserved to be celebrated.

We connected with the community through food drives, neighborhood hot dog cookouts, family fun nights, and more. We invited guests—Olympic gold medalists, authors, singers, and other classes from around the world—to share with our students. We held a "Teach Like a Pirate" day, a book prom, a superhero day (all the teachers dressed up as superheroes and welcomed the kids with a red carpet), a huge reading initiative, and many other events. My teachers learned from some of the best educators in the field: Tony Sinanis, Erin Klein, Tom Murray, Greg Smedley, and Angela Maiers. I worked with my administration to build up our team and continually show them how important they were.

I lead after-school tutoring, Saturday school, and we all pulled small tutoring groups. Every single person on my campus, along with students' parents, worked extremely hard that year. We definitely had trials; it wasn't easy, but I was proud of the work we did.

At the end of the summer of 2015, I sat in a meeting with five other principals from my district to receive the state accountability information for the previous year. Campus accountability is made up of four indexes; campuses that meet the criteria in least three are considered a success. One by one, each principal celebrated his or her campus for meeting either three or all four of the indexes.

Then it was my turn. I flipped open the accountability packet.

One. Just one.

We met just one of the accountability indexes.

I was crushed. I felt destroyed. I felt like every eye was on me and I didn't say another word for the rest of the meeting. I cried the entire way home.

I sent a vox to two of my best friends, Brad Gustafson and Ben Gilpin, both principals in other states, and told them I thought I was done. I clearly didn't know what I was doing. These scores showed I obviously wasn't a good leader. All that work was for nothing.

I've debated long and hard about sharing this story—this side of being an educator. But when I blog, I pride myself on sharing an honest portrayal of education and who I am. I'm passionate about sharing the good as well as the bad. Plus, Ben Gilpin encouraged me to share.

He reminded me this is what a high-stakes accountability system can do. In a matter of seconds, I got lost in the scores and judged my entire year by one day of testing—forgetting the ways we'd touched and changed lives. Now, don't get me wrong. I'm not saying scores aren't

---

I got lost in the scores and judged my entire year by one day of testing —forgetting the ways we'd touched and changed lives.

---

important. They are. But they are only one piece of a school's success—not the only true measure of a "good education."

I know that year was a resounding success. Lives were changed and we made *huge* strides in so many areas those four indexes can never measure. Even though the results sent me reeling, I stood up ready to face another year.

We all have a choice about how we view our situations. It's important to keep a watchful eye on those things we need to improve and find ways to fix them. But it's more important to hold our heads high and not let our failures overwhelm us. Change and growth take time and lots of hard work. We need to continue to work hard and celebrate the successes while building on the failures. Kids deserve it!

Things to Consider and Tweet

1. When have you experienced self-doubt? How did you learn and grow from it?
2. How can you help your colleagues or students learn not to let their failures define them?
3. In what ways can you celebrate others more often?

#KidsDeserveIt

20 Act like a Child

When did we forget what it's like to be a child—to have that sense of wonder, excitement, and joy that defines our every move? Spend any amount of time in a kindergarten classroom and you're quickly reminded of that childlike wonder—endless dreaming, curiosity, and wishful thinking. These kids forgive instantly, run up and greet people with hugs, laugh until their sides hurt, and believe in magic and imaginary friends.

We believe those childlike attitudes are important for adults and need to play a part in the decisions we make. Instead of frowning, saying "no," or focusing on what can't be done, what if we spent more time believing in the impossible? Dreaming the impossible?

Our littlest children believe a cow really can jump over the moon. They hope Santa will bring them gifts, not coal. More significantly, they know they can change the world. And they will—when we either get out of their way or join them on their journey.

How can you tap into your childlike self? How can you begin to tear down the walls of cynicism you've built and begin to dream again? Here are some ideas we've come up with:

1. Take time to just sit and color.
2. Blindfold yourself and let your students lead you through a maze.
3. Find something to laugh at every day.
4. Go out into nature, close your eyes, take in the sounds, and let your imagination run wild.
5. Paint. Draw. Create.
6. Spend time with a group of five-year-olds. Talk to them. Listen to them.
7. Ask a group of students what breaks their hearts, and work together to find solutions. Dream big and utilize their collective and individual genius.
8. Transform your classroom.
9. Call someone you care about and tell them why they're important to you—just because.
10. Forgive quickly—and then move on.
11. Hug someone.
12. Make secret handshakes with students. It'll make both of you smile!
13. Go down the slide at recess. Nobody expects an adult to do that, plus it's lots of fun.
14. Sit on the carpet with students. Being on their level gives you their perspective.

When we choose to act like a child, we see the world in a different light. Our focus changes. Walls begin to fall down and we begin to believe in things we once thought were impossible. We realize what's important and what's not.

Imagine if every educator acted more like a child. Would more kids hold onto their childlike wonder as they grow up?

Remember back to what made you smile and laugh when you were in school. What got you so excited that you'd wake up super early for school? Find the child inside you again and bring that excitement and wonder back! Your kids deserve it!

Find the child inside you again and bring that excitement and wonder back!

Things to Consider and Tweet

1. What are some other ways you can act more like a child?
2. What is the last big dream you had?
3. What happens when we're surrounded by people who've forgotten how to dream?

#KidsDeserveIt

21 Choices and Decisions

Schools don't exist so adults can have jobs. Schools exist for *students*. And your job (and ours) is about making kids feel confident and embracing them for who they are. You can do that by facilitating learning opportunities that empower kids to discover what's possible in this world. By challenging the status quo, you can create deep learning experiences that kids will remember for years to come. In this chapter, we'll share just a few of the ways we've decided to shake things up. We hope what you read here will spark some ideas that you can use in your school.

CRASH COURSE DAY

I (Todd) was looking for a book for our new school staff to read together. Over the summer, I had fallen in love with Kim Bearden's book *Crash Course*. I decided it would be perfect for our fall book study, so I contacted Kim and bought a copy of her book for every staff member at Webb Elementary. When we began reading the book in August, we decided we would be finished reading it and hold a "Crash Course Day" on campus on November 16th. That day would be a time to celebrate and share all we'd learned through the study.

We met weekly to discuss the chapter and as November 16th drew closer, I was in awe of the conversations I was hearing from staff members about the creative things they were planning for our students that day. What the staff did not know is that I had been working with Kim Bearden to get her to surprise them by coming down that day as well!

About two weeks before Crash Course Day, Kim and I broke the news to the staff that she was coming. There were screams, there were tears, but most of all there was excitement. The staff was buzzing.

Then Crash Course Day arrived, and to say I was blown away is an understatement. There were underwater adventures, sensory activities, baking, a *Cloudy with a Chance of Meatballs* station, Thanksgiving feasts, and so much more. Throughout the school, classrooms and hallways had been transformed. The teachers were excited, and the kids were truly wowed. I was so moved by the looks of awe on the kids' faces as they walked through the building that day.

When you create imaginative and engaging lessons grounded in the learning standards, kids are more apt to behave well so they don't miss out.

This was also one of those school days when discipline issues didn't exist. It was one of those days where it was proof that when you create imaginative and engaging lessons grounded in the learning standards, kids are more apt to behave well so they don't miss out.

We all left school that day both completely exhausted and reinvigorated by the power that exists in seeing the wonder in children's eyes as they learn and experience something for the first time. I know the memories from that day will last a lifetime—for the kids, the teachers, and for me.

TEAM KID

When I (Adam) met my wife years ago, one of the first things she told me was that she appreciated I had a "helper" job. For me, being around kids and supporting them was second nature; I had grown up watching my dad teach second and third grades.

Now, after many years of school administration, her words feel profoundly truthful. Being in education is fun, exhausting, impactful, challenging, time consuming, and maddening at times. Through all those ups and downs, having a helping job is extremely rewarding.

There have been *many* times throughout my career in education when I've thought about leaving and exploring new endeavors. Those thoughts come and then they quickly fade, because education is where I belong. I don't want to leave the job to someone else.

The saying "Team Kid" is the core of my belief system. Kids are the reason I do what I do! Even when you know your purpose and understand that it matters, there will be times when you feel as if nothing can go right and that everyone is against you. I know, because I've been there. I also know that during those times, you've got to shake things up.

A few years ago, I was in one of those ruts and decided something big needed to happen. I ordered a Roadrunner costume and wore it during morning drop-off. You can probably guess the reactions of the kids, teachers, and parents. Huge smiles! Quite a few burst into laughter. Did wearing a Roadrunner costume have anything to do with our instructional program at school? No way, but it made people excited about school, and as a result, they wanted to join in and support the school culture of Team Kid. Taking a chance on a little silliness also turned me around and helped me to focus on what was important—supporting the community and having fun!

MATH FAIR

I (Todd) had always loved watching science fairs, but as a math teacher, I was slightly jealous that I could never do that with my kids. Until one day, I thought, *why can't I?* Why not have a math fair? My students and I had recently done a Skype call with Jack Andraka (winner of the Intel International Science and Engineering Fair in 2012) and had gotten a glimpse of his science fair project. They were excited about the idea of participating in a math fair. I sent home a letter explaining the project to the parents, since students would complete it outside of school.

The requirements for the math fair projects were that the students had to choose something in which they were interested and then show at least six different ways math was involved in or related to their topic. Since they could choose anything they wanted, the topics ranged from Skittles, softball, making *queso*, karate, dance, mechanics, Minecraft, and even *The Walking Dead*. They had two weeks to submit their topic to me, but there was a catch: Once someone submitted a topic, that topic was off-limits to anyone else.

After they submitted their topic, they could start working on their project at home. They were told they had to have at least three visuals and six ways math was involved with their topic. They could interpret "visuals" any way they wanted, whether that was making a poster, bringing items, making items, whatever! The point of this project was for students to have fun, share their passions, and show how math is everywhere. The only boundaries were the ones students set for themselves.

The week of the math fair, students practiced their presentations in class. They were fifth graders, and most of them didn't know how to present. So we talked about inflection, voice control, audio, and looking at the audience. Their peers gave positive and constructive feedback as well. It was a great time of learning some important communication skills. By the day of the event, the kids felt prepared. They felt even more confident when they received a "good luck" Tweet from Jack Andraka that day.

We held the math fair on a Thursday evening from six to seven in our cafeteria. Projects with larger (or living) visuals were set up on our bus ramp.

Attending the fair was mandatory for students, who had had more than a month's notice. Out of my seventy-two students, only three did not show up. And we had more than 200 adults attend! (For that rural area, those were GREAT numbers!) We even broadcast the fair live via Ustream (big thanks to my wife, Lissette). Using Ustream also meant that we could record it to share with all the parents and family members who weren't able to attend.

I can honestly say that I have never been more proud of any group of students. These kids impressed me, their family members, and their peers with the amount of work and creativity they put into their projects. Some brought live horses and ponies for their projects. Others made food, did science experiments, and brought relevant items to pass out at their booths.

As I talked and posted about the math fair afterwards, I heard the comments of, "Oh, you can *tell* whose parents helped them." Did some parents help their children? Yes. Can you tell who did and who didn't have help? Yes. But maybe that isn't all bad.

Here's what I mean. After the fair, I talked with a little girl (whose mom clearly had done most of the work) and asked her why she picked the topic she did for her project. I knew it wasn't a topic that truly interested her. Her response will stick with me for a lifetime. She said, "I knew the only way to get my mom to spend time with me was to pick the company she worked for." Wow.

After hearing that, it didn't matter to me if that mom put together the entire project. I can guarantee you that her daughter sat next to her the entire time and spent moments with her mom that she may not have gotten to otherwise. To me, that made everything worth it.

As students showed up for school the next morning, they were *still* talking about how much fun they'd had. I have never seen kids so proud of themselves and the work they put into something. To me, that is the biggest sign of success.

A Decision

Every day is an opportunity to make a decision. What are you going to do? How are you going to act? How are you going to leave your mark? How are you going to believe in your students and support them? Are you going to forgive them and allow a fresh start every day?

How are you going to leave your mark?

Make choices that focus on your students. Remember that school is not about us, it's about them. *Inspire your students.* Let them share what they're passionate about. Look for ways to push them to do better than they ever dreamed. And if you have a random idea, try it out! The outcome may be better than you could imagine. Don't hold back. Make decisions that optimize the most of their time, their opportunity, and their chance. Kids deserve it!

Things to Consider and Tweet

1. How are you making your school the best possible environment for kids?
2. How do you stay focused on kids and on doing what's best for them?
3. How are you pushing yourself to take advantage of every minute?

#KidsDeserveIt

22 Alien Look

I t used to offend us. It used to make us think twice. But now we're so used to it, and we see it as a badge of honor.

It is the "alien" look. If you're trying to innovate, you've likely seen it. You heard a new idea at a conference, through your online connections, or from your Voxer group that you want to try. You'd like to have the support of your colleagues or even your boss, so you mention the idea to them. And they give you that alien look. The stare, the eye roll—maybe a small laugh or snicker. Or maybe nothing at all. When you're talking, they don't make eye contact and the room gets really quiet.

That look can destroy your confidence and make you back down and doubt what you first thought was a killer idea.

Why do people react this way? We're guessing there are a lot of reasons:

- They're afraid.
- They wish it was their idea.
- They feel like you're not following the plan which was developed.
- They'd rather be safe than adventurous.
- *We haven't tested it out yet.*
- They think it means more work for them.
- It's different, new—and it makes them uncomfortable.

Dinner with a Gentleman

Father figures. It's always incredible to me (Todd) how much of an impact men have in children's lives. I can clearly think about the impact two men in particular, my youth pastors Troy Sikes and Nick Shock, had on my life as a youth. I know the power of male role models; I've seen it firsthand. I always want to tap into that for our students.

This year, our school held its very first "Dinner with a Gentleman." When I initially started planning this event, I got that alien look. I had people telling me I was wasting my time, that men wouldn't show up, that we'd never find the money, and so on. I had doubters and negative talkers every step of the way. But I kept pushing.

Now, let me back track a little.

A few months before, we began our Watch DOGS Program. It's a program that seeks to get men involved in volunteering, even one day, at their child's school. We partnered with another elementary school in our community and housed a kick-off event at their campus.

After lots of advertising, talking about it, and offering *free pizza*, our campus had only two (*two!*) father figures show up.

It was crushing.

We all know the value of getting men involved in a child's education and life in general. And it has been a mission that's been heavy on my heart for a while. Especially being raised by a single mother, it made me think about the men who impacted me and are the reason I am who I am today.

I sat down with my assistant principal, Aaron Marvel, and brainstormed. I knew we could do better than just a kick-off event. We thought about the ever-popular Donuts with Dad, but after looking at our mornings here at Webb Elementary and our facilities, it just wouldn't work during a school day. Then (with the help of fellow principals Ben Gilpin, Brad Gustafson, and Adam Welcome) we had an idea. Why not turn this around and find a way to celebrate the men in these kids' lives? Many of my students don't have their fathers in their lives. They have cousins, uncles, brothers, stepfathers, grandfathers, etc. We toyed around with different names for the event, such as "Dinner with Dad," "Dinner with Dudes," and more. We finally settled on "Dinner with a Gentleman."

I found a little money in a Title Fund account that had to be used for parent engagement and involvement, priced out some BBQ (everyone loves BBQ in Texas), and hired a caterer.

After the disappointing showing at the Watch DOGS kick-off event, we were being hopeful in estimating that 150 might show up for a free dinner. I created flyers and talked to each class. I asked students to consider coming and to turn in an RSVP form so we would know how much food and seating we would need. I made sure the kids knew this was a Dinner with a *Gentleman*, so they could invite their grandfathers, uncles, older brothers, family friends—any man who meant something to them.

Well, let's just say we weren't prepared for what came next.

Over the next few weeks, we received 200, then 300, then 400 RSVPs. We didn't have money or seating for that! I called for help from my team, and we brainstormed. We stressed.

We found a new caterer and changed the meal idea (we had to stay on budget!). We contacted some local companies to help us with the funding just in case. We worked with the city, the district, and the VFW to get tables and chairs for our event.

Then we stopped taking reservations three days before the event. At this point, we had 647—yes, 647—RSVPs. We were floored. We had never experienced anything like this before.

We went into frantic planning mode. I reached out to the staff at Webb and asked for help! And, man, they helped.

Centerpieces were made, tables were delivered and set up, and finally, the dinner began and our guests arrived. It took everything in me not to break down at the sight of a room full of men spending time with these children. We had more than 580 actually show up for the event.

When the kids and their gentlemen came in, they got to pick out a book from a table full of choices (we wanted to have them leave with something they could use to continue building relationships). They then found their seats. The first of three carefully chosen guest speakers took the stage. We wanted to make sure we reflected our community and our fathers, so we had speakers of different ethnicities, upbringings, and careers.

We then served our meal and had a panel of students who shared what having a gentleman involved in their lives meant to them. Throughout the evening, a slideshow of kids and music played. And we closed with a song by our music teacher, Mr. Kevin Haliburton.

All in all, it went off without a hitch. I couldn't believe it, but I shouldn't have been surprised. I am surrounded by a team of rock star educators who continually step up and make events like this a success. I am proud of them. Even more so, I am proud of the gentlemen who showed up with their kids. I can only hope that memories were made and relationships were deepened by spending just a little more time together. Children need men involved in their lives (just like they need women).

Was it a risk to try again after such a miserable launch to our Watch DOGS Program? You bet. Could the event have flopped and left us all disappointed? Maybe. But seeing the kids spend time with men who cared enough about them to show up at their school made all the stress and planning well worth the effort and the worry.

Look Ahead, Be Relevant

I (Adam) have talked about cursive and typing for years, and the relevancy they each hold in our schools. The advent of voice typing and voice applications have been on my mind recently. The vast majority of text messages I send are through voice text. Most of my writing happens through Google Docs with their new voice typing feature.

Earlier this year, I started really talking about voice typing and that we need to be showing our kids how to utilize this tool, even more so than typing skills.

I got the alien look. It came from colleagues, directors, other teachers, and even parents.

Today, so many people who work with me are talking about voice typing. How their students are writing so much more than they did when they had to type. Kids still need to edit their writing, of course, but voice typing allows them to get all their ideas down without having to navigate the keyboard, which is challenging for many kids.

I got the alien look. It came from colleagues, directors, other teachers, and even parents.

I take the alien look as a badge of honor. If your idea makes sense, if it helps kids, if it's free, and if you see results, don't worry about what others think of it. New ideas that seem radical are commonly looked down upon. Do what's best for kids and push your relevant ideas!

PUSH FORWARD

Far too many educators back down when they get the alien look. They put their idea away and go back to playing it safe—doing what they've always done. They follow the checklist and do what is easily accepted.

Why? Why don't more of us stand up to those looks? Why don't we challenge the status quo and focus on doing what's best for kids regardless of the consequences? If we don't, we don't push education forward. We don't inspire innovation and creativity. We just get more of the same.

Be glad when you get the alien look. It means you're thinking differently and trying to push the envelope with new ideas. It means even though not every idea will come to fruition, you keep pushing to give kids what's best. Because your kids deserve it!

Things to Consider and Tweet

1. Think about someone in history who probably got the alien look. How would our world be different if he hadn't pushed the envelope?
2. What idea from which you previously backed down are you now ready to try again?
3. How can we challenge kids to think outside the box if we are not doing it ourselves?

#KidsDeserveIt

23 The Battles We Face

We face battles every day. Battles like:

- Not enough money for your school
- Too many initiatives
- Difficulty staying focused
- Team members going in different directions
- Working long hours and spending too much time away from family
- Unrealistic expectations
- Feeling alone and without support
- Being told "no" at every turn
- Questioning the big dreams and ideas you came in with

Sometimes we quickly conquer our battles, but sometimes they drag on for days, weeks, or even years. Sometimes these battles can leave so much collateral damage that we consider leaving the profession. The challenge is to decide how to handle them.

We've learned that battles are easier to deal with when you share your struggles with others. As you talk to others, you discover they are going through the same things, and there's comfort in that. Maybe we get so caught up in our own junk that we don't think about sharing or don't want to "bother" others with our struggles.

Battles are easier to deal with when you share your struggles with others.

But you need to share your battles. When you do, your load is lightened and the biggest wars seem less insurmountable. Plus, it reminds you you're not in this alone. We love the phrase, "What's the easiest way to eat an elephant? Piece by piece."

Finding "our people" has saved both of our careers. Through these connections, we've allowed ourselves to be vulnerable with each other—sharing our hearts, our fears, our failures, our joys, our struggles, our celebrations, and our pain. We challenge each other, but always provide a listening ear and a shoulder. Education is a hard profession. We have to stick together.

We've also learned to focus on what's most important. We must find balance in how we spend our time. We can't forget to take time to do what brings us personal joy and lights our fire—things that have absolutely nothing to do with our school or with education. If we don't find time to disconnect and do something outside of education, we run the risk of burning out.

We must outflank the challenges which take us off course. There will always be battles, but let's remember why we're in this. We're not just fighting the battle for us. We're fighting these battles for the kids—to give kids the very best. Our kids deserve it!

Things to Consider and Tweet

1. What is a battle you've faced recently?
2. How can you support your colleagues?
3. How do you seek out your colleagues for support?

#KidsDeserveIt

24 Take Charge of Your Learning

Education is one of the few professions people enter thinking they've finished their education. Educators graduate from college, ready to tackle the world and thinking they're finished learning. How would you like to visit a doctor who has the same attitude? Maybe she's been practicing for years, but has never updated her research or practices. We don't know about you, but we wouldn't visit her!

So why do we expect parents to put their children in our classrooms if we haven't changed our practices or studied any new research in years? As few as five to ten years ago, educators had to ask permission to attend a training. The district had to find funds and a substitute. Plus, finding time to write sub plans often dissuaded us from attending. The process was complicated and difficult. But we don't live in that world anymore.

Technology puts a limitless world of learning at our fingertips. It requires no money or sub plans, and you don't have to ask permission to attend!

Technology puts a limitless world of learning at our fingertips.

Don't get us wrong, because there's a lot of value in face-to-face conferences and trainings. The conversation and collaboration alone make them valuable. But our point is there are so many more options now. Through social media networks and tools like FaceTime, Google Hangouts, Periscope, Blab, and Voxer, you can connect with, learn from, and grow alongside educators from all over the world—twenty-four hours a day, seven days a week!

We've heard lots of excuses as to why educators don't continue learning. But we haven't heard one yet which makes us say, "Yeah, you're right. I guess ongoing education really isn't important."

I don't have the time. We operate with the belief that we have time for what is important to us. That means time isn't the real issue. We believe ongoing learning should be important to educators. Look at where you are spending your time. Could you change your schedule or invest your time differently to allow for personal and professional development? It doesn't have to take endless hours or be complex. Simply find someone else who is already doing what you want to do, learn from them, and adapt what they're doing to your classroom. Don't reinvent the wheel, just make it better.

The new technology is too confusing. We love hearing educators say this. Why? Because then we get to tell them about this great tool called Google, which is accessible to everyone. When we don't understand something or how to use something, we just Google it. Then we watch a YouTube video or read an article and *teach ourselves.* How often do we tell our kids to figure something out for themselves? Why is it okay for us to tell our kids to do this and not take the time to do the same thing?

My district would never approve it. How many times have you been told "no" when you wanted to do something you thought would make you a better educator or benefit the kids? We've been there—many times. Invest your time learning through online tools which cost the district nothing. Perhaps when your supervisors see how you're growing and how the kids are benefiting from what you're learning, they'll be more likely to approve a future educational opportunity. If not— you're still giving the kids what they deserve!

I don't really understand the value. Too often we hear teachers say they don't see how continued learning will make things better. The value is in learning how you can push boundaries and do great things for kids. With so many resources at your disposal, you can see exactly how "real-life" teachers are making positive impacts on their kids. Learning from them gives you more knowledge and ideas to share with your own kids.

I've been doing fine for years; why change now? Some educators have found versions of success by doing things a particular way. They're very comfortable and don't see any reason to change. The question we always ask is, "If the world was great with no air-conditioning, no TV, or no cars, why was there a reason to change?" Our world changes at a very rapid pace—because it continually finds new ideas to make our lives better. We need to be the same way. If we don't, we may end up like video rental stores and get wiped out by those who are growing and moving ahead.

Our tests scores are already strong. Why push forward when every-thing is good? This is exactly the time to push! One of our favorite say-ings comes from Jim Collins: "Good is the enemy of great." It couldn't be more true when it comes to using test scores as the reason for learn-ing. The misguided thinking is that if scores are good, innovation is unnecessary. If test scores are high, you are safe and you can keep things status quo—comfortable and easy. In truth, test scores give you capital; they allow you to take risks. People who aren't in education trust those test scores. They're a number to point at. Don't allow yourself to make an excuse on why we shouldn't *always* be pushing forward. When test scores are high, that's exactly when you're in a unique position to push harder and try even more out-of-the box ideas.

Excuses. These are all just excuses which slow down change, creativity, and innovation. Ignore the excuses and take charge of your learning. Push to try new things and be better. Your kids deserve it.

Things to Consider and Tweet

1. What are some excuses you've heard people make for not taking charge of their own learning? What excuses have you made yourself?
2. What are some of your favorite tools or resources for continuing your learning?
3. Why do you find it important to keep growing and learning?

#KidsDeserveIt

25 Adults Are Just Big Kids

Some of the best advice we got when we stepped into administration was, "Now you're dealing with adults. You're exceptional at handling children, so remember: Adults are just kids in bigger bodies." At first we laughed at this, but the more we've worked with adults, the more we see it's true.

PRAISE YOUR STAFF AND COWORKERS

The practice of handing out "Hats Off to You" cards (see Chapter 5) changed a lot of things in my (Todd's) school. Our kiddos wanted to be recognized, and be recognized in front of their families. Our families were also changed. Countless parents choked back tears when we called because no one had ever called them to tell them something great about their child.

As I made phone call after phone call, I remembered the advice I'd been given about adults being big kids. And I had an idea: *Why don't we do something like "Hats Off" for adults?* I took the idea and ran with it. But I wanted it to start as a surprise—to be completely unexpected.

In October, I told my school family I was working on a campus project. I sent them a Google Form asking for the addresses and phone numbers of their parents or, for anyone who no longer had parents or were estranged from them, someone else who held a "parent" place in their life.

During the month of December, I wrote cards to each and every family member on the list. I told them their "child" worked at our school and then listed some qualities I appreciated about him or her. I told them how much better our team is because of having their son or daughter on board.

I mailed the cards, timing the delivery during the Christmas break. I wanted the families to have a special Christmas surprise. I got eleven different messages during the break from staff members and their parents, telling me how much this simple act of a card meant to them. I think the parents were impacted more than my staff. Think about it. How often do we receive feedback from our adult children's employer about how much they're appreciated? Not often enough. It needs to happen more.

Imagine how a school could transform with the simple act of sending a letter to recognize adults as well as children. And the letters to parents were only the beginning. Over the next few months, I began to give "Hats Off" cards to the adults on campus as well. They usually received an email or vox asking them to come to my office during their free period or after school. When they came, I'd present them with a "Hats Off" card and told them something I recognized about them. Then I asked them who they wanted me to call. I still love getting the shocked faces of "really"? After I assure them I'm serious, they usually give me their parent's phone number. If you think calling the parent of a fourth grader is exciting, wait until you call the parent of an adult who works on the campus!

There's always that beginning moment of shock. Then I explain to them why I'm calling, how much I appreciate their child, and the great job they did in raising them. There's always some laughing that takes place, sometimes a few tears, and even some "I love yous" are said through the phone between parent and child (because we really are all just big kids).

Think about making random phone calls to the parents of your staff—sharing the awesome things their "children" are doing at your school. If we recognize kids, why can't we recognize adults, too?

And you don't have to be an administrator to do this! You can recognize those with whom you work, people on your team, cafeteria workers—everyone! The idea is to recognize people around you. Remind them how important they are.

Will you have to pay for stamps? Yep. Will your hand hurt from all the writing? Yep. Will it take hours? Yep. Will the positive ripples of this be felt for a long time to come? Absolutely. And that's why we do it—to make the adults in our kids' lives also feel valued. Our kids deserve it!

Recognize people around you. Remind them how important they are.

Things to Consider and Tweet

1. In what creative ways can you recognize the adults in your life?
2. When do you remember being recognized by other adults?
3. When was the last time you felt valued?

#KidsDeserveIt

26 Unplug and Recharge

Educators work far more than an eight-hour workday. Their work is a complicated jigsaw puzzle of time with kids, meetings, trainings, phone calls, emails, letters to write, grades, and so much more. But educators are committed and work tirelessly because they know how much the kids deserve it. They know they only have a small window of time to make a lasting impact on their students.

So we sometimes exhaust ourselves. We get overwhelmed. We burn out. We have seen how quickly burn-out can derail even the best educators. So how do we keep that from happening?

It's important to unplug and recharge. Take time to disconnect from the phone, email, and constant Facebook and Twitter updates. It's hard because those things are constantly pulling at you. But it's important to put them aside sometimes. Spend some time with those closest to you—or even spend some time alone. When you do, you refuel yourself.

Spend some time with those closest to you—or even spend some time alone. When you do, you refuel yourself.

Do things which make you happy—things which have nothing to do with school. Garden, paint, join a theater group, do yoga, or run—the possibilities are limitless! When you choose to take time for yourself, you're taking care of yourself as well, and you become better for kids who deserve the best educator possible.

Turn It Off

When I (Adam) leave school every day, I set my phone so that my work email is turned off. My day is finished—I've been working for ten hours or more—it's time to be with my family. But I had an even bigger idea about unplugging. Honestly, I wasn't sure if I could pull it off, but I took the plunge! I left my iPhone at home when my family and I went to hang out at the beach and relax—for five days!

When I told some people what I was doing, I got lots of shocked responses:

- "Wow, that's bold!"
- "I couldn't do that. It would stress me out not to be connected."
- "How will you know what's going on? How will you find restaurants and other things?"

We're used to checking in on whatever keeps us connected on an hourly (or minute-by-minute) basis. I decided it was time for a break.

Those five days with my wife and children were the best! After about thirty minutes in the car, the muscle memory of "checking my phone" relaxed, and I was completely engaged in our family conversation. Every second in the hotel, at the beach, on a walk, or out for dinner was spent 100 percent engaged! A friend of mine had asked how I would document our trip without my iPhone. I brought my camera! Problem solved!

When we got home I responded to a few text messages, emails, and social media notifications, but I hadn't been bothered one bit by not having my phone with me.

It's so incredibly important for us to remember to take care of ourselves as well as our students. To disconnect from our educational sphere and just be.

So take the plunge! Leave your phone at home and really disconnect. Engage fully with the people around you. Unplug and recharge so you come back to school ready to go! Your kids deserve it!

Things to Consider and Tweet

1. When was the last time you unplugged? What benefits did you see?
2. What is your greatest fear about disconnecting?
3. Why do you think it's important to disconnect?

#KidsDeserveIt

27 More Meat, Less Glitter

We've all seen it. That post, a picture on Pinterest, a Periscope interview, or a shared Facebook link about an incredible, awe-inspiring classroom or teaching idea. It looks bright, shiny, and really cool. But it turns out to be more glitter than substance.

We admit we've fallen victim to the sparkle, too. We saw incredible pictures from someone else's work, but instead of designing a fun lesson full of meat and potatoes, we settled for one with neon and glitter.

Where does that need come from—the need to compare ourselves to others and feel we have to try cutesy ideas to measure up? It's definitely more of an epidemic in elementary than in secondary education. We think it comes down to the need to design a lesson and space in which we're comfortable. We want others to say, "Aw, that's so cute!" or, "Your students must be having so much fun!"

Don't get us wrong. *Fun* is important. If a student doesn't love the learning process, they won't learn anything worth remembering. But we can't focus so much on the glitter—the sparkly, shiny *oooohs* and *ahhhs* of a lesson. We can't focus just on what we want. Fun—even glittery—lessons are great, but they must connect to the curriculum. We must have specific teaching points with relevant outcomes. We must push kids to go deeper in their thinking. There has to be some meat to the lesson.

Hope King, a friend of ours and blogger at *Elementary Shenanigans* is a teacher who does the most outrageous and out-of-the-box lessons. Hope is the queen of transformations—transforming her room into the Arctic Circle or creating Jurassic World. But Hope also keeps the academic content front and center. Everything else revolves around it. If she can't make the content the star of the show in whatever crazy idea she's come up with, she doesn't do the lesson.

We have to do this as well. We can't get caught up in how much fun something looks if learning doesn't also take place. Our students are only with us a short amount of time, and we don't have a minute to waste! Again, this doesn't mean we can't have fun with kids. We just need to keep the focus on learning.

So be creative. Be innovative. Find the most mundane task and come up with an outrageous way to bring the fun into the learning. But be purposeful. Create lessons that, as Dave Burgess says, "Kids are willing to pay to listen to."

Capitalize on every moment of instructional time. Give kids an educational diet which includes more meat and less glitter. Make learning fun—but make it purposeful. Kids deserve it!

Find the most mundane task and come up with an outrageous way to bring the fun into the learning.

Things to Consider and Tweet

1. When have you fallen victim to focusing on glitter more than meat? Why did you do it?
2. How can we encourage teachers to think outside the box, yet keep the activity focused on the content?
3. When did you really push yourself to create something epic which still focused on the content? If you haven't done this, what's holding you back?

#KidsDeserveIt

28 For the Love of Reading

We love to read. We especially love to read to classrooms full of students. As educators, we know the importance of reading and how it affects every single part of a child's education. But how do we instill that love of reading into our students, so it isn't something they do just so they can get points or complete a book report?

Starting a Movement

I (Todd) hated reading until I was in the fifth grade, when I discovered the book series *Animorphs,* by K. A. Applegate. That one little series got me hooked on reading. I still remember my grandmother giving me an index card box and a ton of index cards. Every time I read a book, she would have me write down the title, author, a little blurb about it, and file the card alphabetically in my little box. Then when I would go visit her, she would give me fifty cents for every one completed, and we would use the money to go buy more books! I was hooked!

Though I always taught and loved teaching math, I still tried to instill a love of reading in my students. I even had a class library with more than 200 books. (I still have the library, but now it's in my principal's office.) But for a long time, reading wasn't a top priority or passion for my district's students. Thankfully, my whole team *is* passionate about changing that.

After reading Donalyn Miller's book *The Book Whisperer* during Christmas break one year, I came up with a campus-wide initiative. Here's the message I sent out to staff:

> I've always considered myself a math teacher, even though math was the subject I hated the most in school. I loved reading and writing, but not until I was in the fifth grade. Why? Because I had never found the right book for me. I had always been told what I *had* to read or what we were reading as a class didn't suit me, so I hated reading. It wasn't until middle school that I ran across the *Animorphs* series. Well, sixty or so *Animorphs* books later, I was hooked and have been an avid reader ever since.
>
> If you remember, questions we asked every single staff member were, "Do you consider yourself a reader?" and, "What was the last book you read?" You see, as teachers, we need to continue reading as well. Regardless of how many things are on our plates, we must find the time to continue our learning and to also read the books that our students are reading. That way, reading can evolve from being simply something that we make children do at school to becoming a passion we share with our students.
>
> I just finished reading *The Book Whisperer* on vacation, and it set off ideas in my head about what we can better do as a campus. I recently interviewed the author,

Donalyn Miller, on EduAllStars[1]. I have also chosen *The Book Whisperer* as our first One Staff/One Book study. I would encourage all staff members to immerse themselves in Donalyn's book together.

But this is just the beginning. Reading *The Book Whisperer* together will be the kick-off to a brand new reading initiative that we'll be starting this semester!

Starting in January, we are going to be challenging every single adult and child to read twenty books before the end of the school year. Now, twenty may sound like a lot, especially to students, but it really isn't! These are twenty books that the students can choose. There will be no grade or anything of the sort. No certain Lexile level has to be chosen. We want to encourage students to read, fall in love with reading, and to see all of us reading as well. Now, we all know we will have students who won't reach the twenty-book goal. That's okay! We just want kids to read more than they ever have. For a child who has only read one book on their own during a school year, achieving five will be a huge celebration! But we still want the goal set of twenty for every student.

Here's some things that will happen:

- Every teacher will have a sign on or near their door that advertises the current book the teacher is reading. (Yes, it's okay and encouraged to read the books the kids are reading!)

- There will be a reader-tracking page that will cover the walls of the hallways. Every child and staff member will get his or her own page to document the books they're reading and how close they are to reaching the goal of twenty.

1 http://www.eduallstars.com/edu-all-star-podcast-session-72-donalyn-miller/

- Every morning on the announcements, someone from the staff will share with students what they're reading and why they chose that book. It's another way to advertise great books!

- Over time, we will begin having students come on the announcements and share the book they're reading or just read. So pay attention to your kiddos! If they've fallen in love with a book, have them come share it with me and we'll let them share on the announcements!

- We will have celebrations for every five books a child reads, so after your student reads five books, please send them to me to celebrate!

- After students have finished a book, they will add it to their goal sheet. There is no book report required, no project, and no form to fill out. Children should spend their time reading, not creating a huge report or project that takes longer to complete than reading the actual book.

- Every morning after you pick up your students, until the announcements come on, ALL students should be reading. We will also be asking them to read during morning breakfast and at bus dismissal. That means your students *need books*! If you haven't taken them to get books or checked if they have any, you need to do so!

- Every classroom needs a class library. Doesn't matter what subject you teach. So start collecting books now that your students can choose from!

- When you send your students to interventions, they need to bring a book with them.

- As students start getting closer to their twenty-book goal, I will begin meeting with them to find out who their favorite authors and books are so I can set up Skypes, Google Hangouts, and find other ways to collaborate with the authors of those books.

- As students finish a book, please send them to the office with that book so I can take a picture of them for our reading wall that we will be creating and for our Twitter and Facebook.

- Find time throughout the day to give students time to read independently. For many of our students, reading at home right away may not be a realistic expectation. We have to let them see the importance of independent reading time at school first.

- Different staff members may be contacting you to set up a time when they can come in and read a short story with your class or share a personal book recommendation. The kids *love* that.

Reading affects every single aspect of our lives and every subject taught at school. It is of the utmost importance and must be treated that way. Students *do not* learn how to read, nor do they fall in love with reading from worksheets or by reading passages. They need to practice reading on their own with a book or story they've fallen in love with, not one that has been assigned to them. Let's work together to build this love of reading in each and every one of our kids! They deserve it!

When we launched the reading initiative schoolwide, the kids ate it up! We covered a huge wall in our cafeteria with photos of kids with their books after they finished them. We had students coming to the announcements to share the book they were reading with the school. We had teachers celebrating and advertising books by each of their doors. I had countless students come "check out" books from my office library. Kids were reading during both breakfast and dismissal. They were *reading* and falling in love with it! And *that* was the point.

Reading to Classes

I (Adam) will admit that when I was younger, I didn't like to read. The crazy thing is, my father was a second-grade teacher. Books were *all* over our house, my parents read to us nightly, and my dad had a huge bookshelf with more than 1,000 books.

My reading passion didn't start until I discovered Roald Dahl in third grade. That's when my literacy journey began. With my own past deeply seeded in my brain, I've always had a special mission as a teacher and principal to help reluctant readers. I really believe that if you develop the reading passion at an early age, it has a much higher probability to stay with you for a lifetime.

Reading is important, really important, especially with kids. Four years ago, I started reading to classes—specifically, I would read the same book to each class on a monthly basis. After I've read my monthly book to each class, I always donate it to our school library.

Four years later, kids now ask me on a daily basis when I'm going to come in and read. Kids and parents are always recommending books to me, which is super fun. Admittedly, I have pretty high standards for my book choices and tend to find stories that align with our Student of the Month themes. Reading with students allows for amazing conversations and for great follow-up lessons led by teachers.

Since that first day reading, I've become a reading principal, and reading to classes is hands down the most influential action I do as a principal.

Reading to classes is hands down the most influential action I do as a principal.

Just Keep Reading

Reading is a fundamental skill. It is one that must be practiced and utilized. We can no longer treat our school like a place where reading only happens during a certain class period or predetermined time.

Our students must also see us reading. They have to see us falling in love with books too, regardless of what our role is on campus.

Some ways that you can do that are:

- Offer to read to a classroom during your break or free period.
- Advertise the book you're reading.
- Create book trailers; or better yet, have the students create them!
- Create a classroom library full of all sorts of things kids can read.
- Let your students go and read to other classrooms (huge confidence booster for those struggling readers when they find "their book").
- Connect with a different grade-level classroom and make reading buddies.

- Dress up as a book character one day.

- Bring in guest readers from the community.

- Use silly voices and exaggerated movements when you read to your class.

- Record yourself reading a book and upload it for others to use or for your kids to hear.

Things to Consider and Tweet

1. Do you consider yourself a reader? If not, what's holding you back? How can you better model for your students?
2. What are some great things you've done to instill a love of reading in kids?
3. What are some of your favorite books to read with or to kids?

#KidsDeserveIt

29 Send Them Home

Every school sends something home with students. For some schools, it's homework. For others, it's library books and textbooks. But the one thing we don't see much of is technology going home.

Why is that?

Is it because we don't trust our kids? We think they'll lose it, break it, or steal it? What is our fear?

Releasing Fear

I (Adam) started sending our Spheros (robotic droids that can be programed with an iPad) home with kids last August. Parents couldn't believe it and the kids were astounded!

I bought a bunch of Spheros for my school to use with the coding class that I teach every Tuesday morning. After watching the kids in action with the Spheros, a thought came to me. *Why don't I send the Spheros home with the kids?*

Crazy, right? I mean, what educator thinks it's a "good" idea to send expensive tech home with their students?

But I didn't care. I saw the excitement in these kids' eyes, and I'm always talking about real-world experiences, so I decided that I'd better put my words into action.

All the kids needed at home was an iPad, and I knew most of my students had one at home. If they didn't, I sent one with them!

I decided to Instagram a photo of our Sphero cart and told parents they could check them out. Literally thirty minutes after my post, I had several parents message me and come by the office to check out a Sphero. I wrote down three different apps the kids can use for Sphero on an index card and gave it to them when they checked it out!

What did the kids do for hours when they got home? They played with the Sphero! Parents posted their own Instagram photos of the Spheros in action, and it was then that I knew we had something big! Kids were learning to code, problem solve, collaborate, and design. When they got frustrated with it and then solved the problem, they were thinking, being creative, and oh, so much more!

No Excuses

We have found that when you relinquish some of the control, stop making excuses, and trust kids just a little, they'll always surprise you. No, it won't be without its hiccups, but it will still be awesome!

Many students with whom we've worked don't have some of the "fancy" tools we have at school. Things like Chromebooks, Spheros, littleBits, Osmos, and more. They use them in just the predetermined educational settings that we've designed, and that's it. What could they really do with some of the tools in their own environments that would surprise even us?

Imagine what would happen if you gave kids a device and a few specials apps to check out and let them explore over the weekend! Or start an after-school club. Invite kids to share about the tools they're using or things they're designing or creating.

You know what else happens when you send home devices? You create a mindset of trust with your students and families. You're telling them, "We want to break down the walls of our classrooms and

---

When you relinquish some of the control, stop making excuses, and trust kids just a little, they'll always surprise you.

---

become partners in the journey. We trust you enough to send devices that we purchased home with you." It really does begin to eliminate boundaries and preconceived notions. You're telling them, "We want you to take the devices home, learn on your own time, and then come back to school and share that knowledge!"

It's really that easy! You can do it! So many others already are, and we know you can, too!

But some of you may be thinking, "Well, that's nice, but we don't have money to buy devices." And we get that. We've worked, and are still working in environments where money can be hard to find. But that's when you do what teachers do best—problem solve. You get creative.

One of our favorite resources is DonorsChoose.org. Donors Choose allows you to create funding pages to get some of the tools or resources you'd like for your class. It's easy to start and even easier to publicize. We have received thousands of dollars of materials just by asking, and so have our teachers. The worst anyone can ever say is, "No."

The most important thing to remember is this doesn't take long to set up and get going at your school. Is it a little scary? Sometimes. Will some devices and tools get lost or broken? Of course! But that's part of life! We take each situation as it comes. The best you can do is teach kids how to use tools appropriately and respect them, and watch the kids surprise you.

Talk about inspiration: Send them home with your teachers, too. That's where they become experts! Send home the Spheros, the drones, the tablets, and the Chromebooks. Send home the power to explore, imagine, and create.

Things to Consider and Tweet

1. What has held you back from sending technology home? What about your campus/district?
2. What are some ways you could convince others to take that leap?
3. Have you sent things home? What has your experience been?

#KidsDeserveIt

30 Final Thoughts

The ideas and opinions we shared in this book came from our desire to have more educators involved in a conversation we are already having. We've connected with so many in the world of education who want to make a bigger impact. Educators get frustrated with the system they're in—frustrated by getting shut down and being told "no"—again and again and again. Too many are stuck in a rut, walking in a straight line, and afraid to step out and forge a new path. We've met educators surrounded by people who make excuses, talk about why kids can't do things, and are comfortable with *boring*.

If you're not careful, this can suck your soul and make you want to leave education. Our dream for *Kids Deserve It!* is that it will flip the conversation and remind people they're not alone. A huge (and growing) group is starting the conversation, pushing the boundaries, and challenging the status quo—no matter what the consequences may be.

We want to drown out the voices seeking to keep us in our boxes. We want to decrease the many negative stories about education and magnify the risk-takers, the dreamers, those who don't accept "no" for an answer, and those who continuously do what's best for kids.

In the end, we want everything we do to come back to kids. We hope this book has made you think, challenged a few misconceptions, and maybe even encouraged you to step out and be *brave*. The kids don't need just a few of us fighting for them; they need *all* of us fighting for them. Now is your time. We don't have another moment to waste. Why? Because the *Kids Deserve It!*

Acknowledgments

TODD

I would first like to thank my wife, Lissette. She has the patience and compassion of a saint and has given me endless support and encouragement to pursue my dreams.

I would like to thank my students across the years. They have truly taught me everything I know and they are what fuels my fire to continue going on in this profession.

I would also like to thank my team at Webb Elementary and Navasota ISD. They inspire me and challenge me every day. Without the support of my team, I would not be half as good as I seem. But my family at Webb brings everything together just perfectly. Every team member, working tirelessly day after day, helps make this school something worth coming to every day. We have the best team in the country.

I would also like to acknowledge all those who've helped shape who I am. My youth pastors, Troy Sikes and Nick Shock. My friend with whom I started this whole "social media" and Ninja journey, Stacey Huffine, and my former colleagues at Waller ISD.

To Ben Gilpin, Brad Gustafson, and Chris Pombonyo, who have changed my life forever and continue to be my sounding boards and voices of encouragement. For years now, you guys have helped me through some of the toughest times in my life and never judged or abandoned me. I am forever grateful for your brotherhood.

I must acknowledge Troy Mooney, without whom I don't know if I ever would have taken the leap into social media that changed my life.

My family. They laugh with me, they argue with me, and they encourage me. They do what a family should. Thank you to my mom and dad who have always had my back. Without parents like mine, I wouldn't be where I am today.

To Dave and Shelley Burgess, who had the faith in us from the start. You encouraged us to be ourselves and helped us find our voice. This book happened because you took a chance. You two went from being our EduHeroes, to our friends, to our publishers, and so much more. I can't wait to see what the future holds.

And finally to Adam. Never would I have expected to meet my BFAM (brother from another mother) randomly at a conference and see my whole world flipped upside down in a good way. This book would have never happened without you. On a daily (if not hourly) basis, you push me to be better. You remind me of who I am and what I am fighting for. You encourage me and have treated me and my family like your own. This friendship and partnership is one I never saw coming, but was truly a gift from God. Thank you for going on this journey with me, allowing me to be myself, and to never settle. This book, and *Kids Deserve It!* in general, is a true reflection of the partnership and like-mindedness we have in each other. There's no one else with whom I'd rather go on this journey!

ADAM

I have many people to thank and acknowledge, but no two people have made me the educator and person I am today other than my dad and mom. My dad (Bob Repicky) taught second and third grades for 35+ years. Seeing him in action with students, encouraging them, being innovative, and telling them that they could succeed has made me the educator I am today. Thank you for all the inspiration and motivation, Dad. I miss you very much and wish you were here to read this book! To my mom (Maureen Abshire), thank you for always pushing me, believing in me, and loving me no matter what!

My wife (Stacy) and two children (Greta and Tilden) for providing daily laughter, love, smiles, and so many amazing memories that we're creating together—I love you all very much.

To my first "teacher coach" when I was a fifth-grade teacher: Kim Hamill, you held my hand and then pushed me down a path to success. I still value our friendship in so many ways. Thanks for all you've done.

To Leslie Anderson and Nadine Rosenzweig, who've really coached me to be the principal I am today: Having two strong, passionate, talented, experienced, and focused women leaders in my life has shaped me in so many fabulous ways!

Thank you to all my students from over the years who have made me a better teacher and human being. For getting in contact with me many years later so we can connect, laugh, and talk about the next leg of your journey!

Of course Todd—Twitter brought us together and then our passion for education solidified that one evening in Long Beach at dinner with Remind. Writing with you has been such an enjoyable journey: our friendship together, laughing and crying together, and always doing what's best for kids. Thank you, my friend, for writing a book with me!

Connect with Us!

TODD
toddnesloney.com

ADAM
adamwelcome.blogspot.com

KDI
KidsDeserveIt.com
#KidsDeserveIt
@KidsDeserveIt
www.facebook.com/kidsdeserveit

DAVE BURGESS
Consulting, inc.

Teach Like a PIRATE

*Increase Student Engagement, Boost Your
Creativity, and Transform Your Life as an Educator*
By Dave Burgess (@BurgessDave)

Teach Like a PIRATE is the New York Times'
best-selling book that has sparked a worldwide
educational revolution. It is part inspirational
manifesto that ignites passion for the profession
and part practical road map, filled with dynamic
strategies to dramatically increase student
engagement. Translated into multiple languages,
its message resonates with educators who want
to design outrageously creative lessons and transform school into a life-changing experience for students.

Learn Like a PIRATE

*Empower Your Students to Collaborate,
Lead, and Succeed*

By Paul Solarz (@PaulSolarz)

Today's job market demands that students be
prepared to take responsibility for their lives and
careers. We do them a disservice if we teach them
how to earn passing grades without equipping
them to take charge of their education. In Learn
Like a Pirate, Paul Solarz explains how to design
classroom experiences that encourage students
to take risks and explore their passions in a stim-
ulating, motivating, and supportive environment
where improvement, rather than grades, is the focus. Discover how student-led
classrooms help students thrive and develop into self-directed, confident citizens
who are capable of making smart, responsible decisions, all on their own.

P is for PIRATE

Inspirational ABC's for Educators

By Dave and Shelley Burgess (@Burgess_Shelley)

Teaching is an adventure that stretches the imagination and calls for creativity every day! In *P is for Pirate*, husband and wife team, Dave and Shelley Burgess, encourage and inspire educators to make their classrooms fun and exciting places to learn. Tapping into years of personal experience and drawing on the insights of more than seventy educators, the authors offer a wealth of ideas for making learning and teaching more fulfilling than ever before.

Play Like a Pirate

Engage Students with Toys, Games, and Comics

by Quinn Rollins

Yes! School can be simultaneously fun and educational. In *Play Like a Pirate*, Quinn Rollins offers practical, engaging strategies and resources that make it easy to integrate fun into your curriculum. Regardless of the grade level you teach, you'll find inspiration and ideas that will help you engage your students in unforgettable ways.

eXPlore Like a Pirate

Gamification and Game-Inspired Course Design to Engage, Enrich, and Elevate Your Learners

By Michael Matera (@MrMatera)

Are you ready to transform your classroom into an experiential world that flourishes on collaboration and creativity? Then set sail with classroom game designer and educator, Michael Matera, as he reveals the possibilities and power of game-based learning. In *eXPlore Like a Pirate*, Matera serves as your experienced guide to help you apply the most motivational techniques of gameplay to your classroom. You'll learn gamification strategies that will work with and enhance (rather than replace) your current curriculum and discover how these engaging methods can be applied to any grade level or subject.

Pure Genius

Building a Culture of Innovation and
Taking 20% Time to the Next Level

By Don Wettrick (@DonWettrick)

For far too long, schools have been bastions of boredom, killers of creativity, and way too comfortable with compliance and conformity. In *Pure Genius*, Don Wettrick explains how collaboration—with experts, students, and other educators—can help you create interesting, and even life-changing, opportunities for learning. Wettrick's book inspires and equips educators with a systematic blueprint for teaching innovation in any school.

The Zen Teacher

Creating FOCUS, SIMPLICITY, and TRANQUILITY in
the Classroom

By Dan Tricarico (@TheZenTeacher)

Teachers have incredible power to influence—even improve—the future. In *The Zen Teacher*, educator, blogger, and speaker Dan Tricarico provides practical, easy-to-use techniques to help teachers be their best—unrushed and fully focused—so they can maximize their performance and improve their quality of life. In this introductory guide, Dan Tricarico explains what it means to develop a Zen practice—something that has nothing to do with religion and everything to do with your ability to thrive in the classroom.

140 Twitter Tips for Educators

Get Connected, Grow Your Professional
Learning Network, and Reinvigorate Your Career

By Brad Currie, Billy Krakower, and Scott Rocco (@bradmcurrie, @wkrakower, @ScottRRocco)

Whatever questions you have about education or about how you can be even better at your job, you'll find ideas, resources, and a vibrant network of professionals ready to help you on Twitter. In *140 Twitter Tips for Educators*, #Satchat hosts and founders of Evolving Educators, Brad Currie, Billy Krakower, and Scott Rocco offer step-by-step instructions to help you master the basics of Twitter, build an online following, and become a Twitter rock star.

The Innovator's Mindset

Empower Learning, Unleash Talent,
and Lead a Culture of Creativity

By George Couros (@gcouros)

The traditional system of education requires students to hold their questions and compliantly stick to the scheduled curriculum. But our job as educators is to provide new and better opportunities for our students. It's time to recognize that compliance doesn't foster innovation, encourage critical thinking, or inspire creativity—and those are the skills our students need to succeed. In *The Innovator's Mindset*, George Couros encourages teachers and administrators to empower their learners to wonder, to explore—and to become forward-thinking leaders.

50 Things You Can Do with Google Classroom

By Alice Keeler and Libbi Miller
(@AliceKeeler, @MillerLibbi)

It can be challenging to add new technology to the classroom, but it's a must if students are going to be well-equipped for the future. Alice Keeler and Libbi Miller shorten the learning curve by providing a thorough overview of the Google Classroom App. Part of Google Apps for Education (GAfE), Google Classroom was specifically designed to help teachers save time by streamlining the process of going digital. Complete with screenshots, *50 Things You Can Do with Google Classroom* provides ideas and step-by-step instructions to help teachers implement this powerful tool.

Master the Media

How Teaching Media Literacy Can
Save Our Plugged-in World

By Julie Smith (@julnilsmith)

Written to help teachers and parents educate the next generation, *Master the Media* explains the history, purpose, and messages behind the media. The point isn't to get kids to unplug; it's to help them make informed choices, understand the difference between truth and lies, and discern perception from reality. Critical thinking leads to smarter decisions—and it's why media literacy can save the world.

Ditch That Textbook

Free Your Teaching and Revolutionize
Your Classroom

By Matt Miller (@jmattmiller)

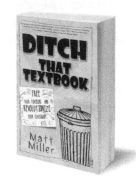

Textbooks are symbols of centuries-old edu-cation. They're often outdated as soon as they hit students' desks. Acting "by the textbook" implies compliance and a lack of creativity. It's time to ditch those textbooks—and those text-book assumptions about learning! In *Ditch That Textbook*, teacher and blogger Matt Miller encour-ages educators to throw out meaningless, pedes-trian teaching and learning practices. He empow-ers them to evolve and improve on old, standard teaching methods. *Ditch That Textbook* is a support system, toolbox, and manifesto to help educators free their teaching and revolutionize their classrooms.

Your School Rocks...So Tell People!

Passionately Pitch and Promote the
Positives Happening on Your Campus

By Ryan McLane and Eric Lowe
(@McLane_Ryan, @EricLowe21)

Great things are happening in your school every day. The problem is, no one beyond your school walls knows about them. School principals Ryan McLane and Eric Lowe want to help you get the word out! In *Your School Rocks...So Tell People!*, McLane and Lowe offer more than seventy imme-diately actionable tips along with easy-to-follow instructions and links to video tutorials. This prac-tical guide will equip you to create an effective and manageable communication strategy using social media tools. Learn how to keep your students' families and community connected, informed, and excited about what's going on in your school.

How Much Water Do We Have?

5 Success Principles for Conquering Any Change and Thriving in Times of Change

by Pete Nunweiler with Kris Nunweiler

In *How Much Water Do We Have?* Pete Nunweiler identifies five key elements—information, planning, motivation, support, and leadership—that are necessary for the success of any goal, life transition, or challenge. Referring to these elements as the 5 Waters of Success, Pete explains that like the water we drink, you need them to thrive in today's rapidly paced world. If you're feeling stressed out, overwhelmed, or uncertain at work or at home, pause and look for the signs of dehydration. Learn how to find, acquire, and use the 5 Waters of Success—so you can share them with your team and family members.

The Classroom Chef

Sharpen your lessons. Season your classes. Make math meaningful.

By John Stevens and Matt Vaudrey (@Jstevens009, @MrVaudrey)

In *The Classroom Chef*, math teachers and instructional coaches John Stevens and Matt Vaudrey share their secret recipes, ingredients, and tips for serving up lessons that engage students and help them "get" math. You can use these ideas and methods as-is, or better yet, tweak them and create your own enticing educational meals. The message the authors share is that, with imagination and preparation, every teacher can be a Classroom Chef.

About the Authors

Todd Nesloney

Todd Nesloney is a learner at heart who has been fortunate enough to spend his entire career doing what he loves. He is currently serving as the principal and lead learner at Webb Elementary in Navasota, Texas. Prior to working in this capacity, Todd served for a year as principal at Navasota Intermediate, and has taught in the fourth and fifth grades for seven years at Fields Store Elementary in Waller, Texas.

Todd has been recognized with several accolades as well. He was the 2015 BAMMY Award recipient for Elementary Principal of the Year and the 2014 BAMMY Award recipient for Classroom Teacher of the Year. Todd has been recognized by President Barack Obama and the White House as a Champion of Change. He was also selected by the National School Board Association as one of the "20 to Watch" in the nation for education and selected by the Center for Digital Education as one of the "Top 40 Innovators in Education." Todd was also recognized by the Texas Computer Education Association as their Elementary Teacher of the Year.

Todd spends his time working to challenge traditional definitions and expectations, all while being completely hands-on with his team and students. In addition to his career as an administrator and educator, Todd also travels, leads staff development, and gives keynote speeches across the country.

Todd is the author of the children's book *Spruce & Lucy* and co-author of the book *Flipping 2.0: Practical Strategies for Flipping Your Class.* Todd is also the co-host of the education podcast series *Kids Deserve It!* and *EduAllStars.*

In his time off, Todd loves to go to the movies, read, garden outside, and spend time with his wife, Lissette.

You can learn more about Todd by visiting his website www.toddnesloney.com or connecting with him on Twitter: @TechNinjaTodd.

Adam Welcome

Adam Welcome has been around education his entire life, growing up in his dad's second-grade classroom from a very young age. Adam taught third, fourth, and fifth grades for seven years. He has been an elementary school principal in the Bay Area for the past six years.

Adam was nominated for Technology Leader of the Year by *Tech & Learning* magazine in 2010, was recognized as Principal of the Year in 2013 for his ACSA Region 6, winner of the East Bay CUE Site Leader of the Year in 2016, and most recently was selected by the National School Board Association as a "20 To Watch" in the nation.

Adam is constantly inspired by helping other educators with finding that "just right" picture book to read with kids, getting them connected on social media, showing principals how to run their school from their phone, and playing quarterback or knock-out at recess.

Adam also loves to blog and has written numerous posts for *EdWeek*, *NAESP* magazine, *ACSA* magazine, and writes his own blog on an almost daily basis.

In his spare time, Adam runs 30-40 miles per week and also three marathons a year. His most favorite activity, though, is hanging out at Lake Tahoe with his wife, Stacy, and two children, Greta and Tilden, where they hike, ski, and just simply enjoy the outdoors.

You can read more of Adam's blogging at adamwelcome.blogspot. com and also connect with him on Twitter and Voxer: @awelcome

CPSIA information can be obtained
at www.ICGtesting.com
Printed in the USA
LVHW05s0747110518
576790LV00006B/7/P